Twayne's United States Authors Series

EDITOR OF THIS VOLUME

Kenneth E. Eble

University of Utah

Rachel Crothers

TUSAS ~~322~~

3 3 2

Rachel Crothers

RACHEL CROTHERS

By LOIS C. GOTTLIEB

University of Guelph

TWAYNE PUBLISHERS

A DIVISION OF G. K. HALL & CO., BOSTON

Published in 1979 by Twayne Publishers,
A Division of G. K. Hall & Co.
All Rights Reserved

Printed on permanent/durable acid-free paper and bound in the
United States of America

First Printing

Library of Congress Cataloging in Publication Data

Gottlieb, Lois C
Rachel Crothers.

(Twayne's United States authors series ;
TUSAS ~~322~~ 332
Bibliography: p.
Includes index.
1.   Crothers, Rachel, 1878–1958
—Criticism and interpretation.
PS3505.R895Z68   812'.5'2   78-20974
ISBN 0-8057-7222-7

For my parents
James and Frieda Cohen

Contents

About the Author

Lois C. Gottlieb received her B.A. from Sophie Newcomb College, her M.A. from Columbia, and her Ph.D. from the University of Michigan. She has taught at Eastern Michigan University, at Wayne State University, at Concordia University in Montreal, and is presently at the University of Guelph. Her scholarly articles and reviews have appeared in *Atlantis, Canadian Newsletter of Research on Women, Canadian Review of American Studies, Michigan Academician, Quarterly Journal of Speech, University of Michigan Papers in Women's Studies* and elsewhere. She co-edited "Women Writers of the Commonwealth," a special issue of *World Literature Written in English* (April 1978).

Preface

Rachel Crothers worked in the American theater, writing plays, directing them, acting, teaching others how to act, for all but twenty of her eighty years, from her earliest juvenile efforts in the 1880s to her latest reported script in 1950. Crothers is a unique figure in the history of American drama because she was a woman playwright, consciously focusing on the lives of women in her plays, and taking a director's role in the production of her dramas at a time when directing in America was an infant enterprise. During her most productive and successful decades, from 1894 to 1937, Crothers saw more than thirty of her plays open in New York, first as the writings of a promising unknown; later, as the expected and welcomed contributions of a seasoned professional. A study of Crothers's plays reaps a double harvest for the student of American drama and for the student of American social history. The evolution of Crothers's dramatic progress reflects many of the major developments of modern American drama, and her plays, as a coherent body of work, reflect decades of American social life subjected to a variety of modern stresses, for which the theater is a natural medium of expression.

Crothers's career demonstrates the conjunction of the right woman at the right moment. She began to make her mark in the theater at a time when increasing opportunities for women in all spheres of educational, professional, and public life were a legacy of the pre-World War I Women's Movement. In her early work, principally in her social problem dramas, her plays explore the injustices and tensions felt by women who were inhabiting an old order of "separate spheres" for the sexes while fighting for a new order of "mixed spheres." In her later work, principally in her sophisticated social comedies, Crothers focuses on the new dilemma for women—the internal conflicts they encountered in the wake of their progress.

The major aims of this book have been to provide an accurate and comprehensive survey of Crothers's career as dramatist; to trace the major developments in her themes and forms in each phase of her career through analysis of some of the best, most interesting, or most significant of her plays; and to supply an American theatrical context as a frame for discussing each phase of her career. In order to achieve these aims, the book is organized chronologically; the chapter divisions suggest meaningful phases of development in Crothers's career and identifiable stages in the evolution of American drama.

The method of analyzing the plays is two-fold. From an historical perspective, I seek to identify what is theatrically conventional in Crothers's dramas and to show how the plays reflect the social concerns of their times. I also discuss the marks of Crothers's individual style, which include her particular treatment of social concerns. From a critical perspective, I give primary attention to the elements of drama that emerge from a reading of the texts: character, action, pattern of conflict, setting, dialogue, theme and mode are described, interpreted and evaluated. I give only brief attention to how Crothers's dramas work as theater. Early in her career Crothers began to, direct her plays; over the years she came to know intimately her stage, her performers, and her audience. Although a theatrical approach to Crothers's plays would be worth taking, it is outside the scope of this study.

Secondary aims of the book have been to inquire more systematically than has been done previously into the nature of the feminism expressed in Crothers's plays and to weigh the critical disagreements about the quality of her dramas.

In order to understand the dramatic feminism in Crothers's plays, I have supplemented critical reaction over the decades on this subject with Crothers's comments on the expression of feminism, or antifeminism, in her plays as well as on her own feminist beliefs and practices. Further, my analysis of the plays' characters and themes consistently considers the questions of whether and how the plays treat feminism.

In dealing with the question of Crothers's critical reputation, my procedure has been to provide a representative sample of the numerous reviews available for almost every play, as well as to take account of the relatively few critical or scholarly treatments of her dramas. Crothers's connection with Broadway has left an indelibly negative imprint on her reputation, yet major critical disagreements arise between those who judged Crothers among the innovative and significant modern American playwrights and those who patronized or condemned her as a successful formula dramatist.

The underlying premise of this study is that Crothers's appropriate place in the history of American drama is not as America's most successful woman dramatist but as an eminent playwright. She exemplifies the important mainstream tradition of American theater, and her unique focus on women's lives over four decades has given lasting works which must be represented in the history of American dramatic literature.

LOIS C. GOTTLIEB

University of Guelph
Guelph, Ontario

Acknowledgments

The following publishers and libraries granted permission to reprint from the works and collections indicated:

Illinois State University, Milner Library, Special Collections: From the Rachel Crothers Scrapbook.

New York Public Library Theatre Collection: From the Robinson Locke Scrapbooks and the Clipping File on Rachel Crothers.

Prentice-Hall, Inc.: From *He and She* by Rachel Crothers in Arthur Hobson Quinn, *Representative American Plays*, (c) 1953. Reprinted by permission of Prentice-Hall, Inc., Englewood Cliffs, New Jersey.

Random House, Inc.: From *Susan and God*, by Rachel Crothers, copyright 1937.

Withers Public Library and Information Center: From the Crothers file.

I'd like to thank several people who were especially helpful at various stages of this project. Bernice Lieberman, of the University of Illinois Library, Champagne-Urbana, provided useful suggestions for verifying early biographical information on Crothers. Katharine Nesteby, Charline Alexander, and the staff of the Information Center at Bloomington (Illinois) Public Library (Withers Public Library and Information Center), generously tracked down many articles and other material about Rachel Crothers's life and career. Robert Sokan, Special Collections Librarian at the Milner Library, Illinois State University, gave substantial help in locating sources of information. Anne Sheffield, New York City, Literary Executrix of the Estate of Rachel Crothers, gave me access to her personal Crothers collection and granted permission to use letters and other documents in various collections of Crothers material.

I am grateful to research grants from Wayne State University and the University of Guelph, which helped to finance portions of this project.

Special thanks of different sort go to my husband, Ben, and my son, Evan. They provided a community of support and encouragement to lighten the task of writing this book.

Chronology

1878   Rachel Crothers born December 12 in Bloomington, Illinois, youngest daughter of Dr. Eli Kirk Crothers and Marie Depew Crothers.

1883   Dr. Marie Depew Crothers received her degree of Doctor of Medicine from the Woman's Medical College of Pennsylvania and returned to Bloomington to establish her own practice.

1891   Graduated from Illinois State Normal University High School.

1892   Graduated from the New England School of Dramatic Instruction in Boston after one term.

1893   Death of her father.

1896–   Moved to New York to gain a foothold in the theater.
1897

1897–   Connected with Stanhope-Wheatcroft school of acting,
1902   first as a student, then as a teacher.

1897   Made New York acting debut with E. H. Sothern's company.

1899   Amateur production of *Criss-Cross* and other one-act plays written for drama-school students.

1906   Professional New York production of *The Three of Us.*

1907   Traveled to London to supervise production of *The Three of Us*, starring Ethel Barrymore.

1908   Production of *Myself Bettina.* Star Maxine Elliott gave Crothers first opportunity to stage and direct her own play.

1910   Production of *A Man's World.*

1911–   Failure of *He and She (The Herfords)* to survive provincial
1912   tryouts.

1914   Publicly disclaims that *Young Wisdom* was intended as an antifeminist play.

1917–   Founded and led Stage Women's War Relief.
1920

1918   Production of *A Little Journey,* starring Estelle Winwood. From this point on, Crothers assumed complete supervision of the staging of all her plays.

1920 Unsuccessful New York revival of *He and She,* starring Rachel Crothers.

1921 Production of *Nice People,* starring Tallulah Bankhead, Katherine Cornell, and Francine Larrimore.

1923 Production of *Mary the Third.*

1924 Production of *Expressing Willie,* with Chrystal Herne.

1929 Production of *Let Us Be Gay;* began Crothers's long association with producer John Golden.

1931 Production of *As Husbands Go.*

1932 Founded and led the Stage Relief Fund.

1932 Production of *When Ladies Meet.* Awarded the Megrue Prize in Comedy in 1933.

1933 Elected to the National Institute of Arts and Letters.

1934– Spent several months in Hollywood writing film scripts.
1935

1937 Production of *Susan and God,* starring Gertrude Lawrence. Cited by Theater Club as the season's most outstanding play.

1939 Awarded the National Achievement Award for 1938 in a White House ceremony.

1940– Founded and led American Theater Wing for War Relief.
1945 Organized Stage Door Canteen in New York.

1940 Produced and directed Paul Vincent Carroll's *The Old Foolishness.*

1941 Honored by Drama Study Club for the year's most distinguished service to the theater.

1945 Withdrew *Bill Comes Back* before production.

1950 Withdrew *My South Window* before production.

1958 Died July 6.

1973 Revival of *He and She* by Washington Area Feminist Theater.

CHAPTER 1

The Apprentice Years

I Bloomington Beginnings

RACHEL Crothers was born in 1878 into an eminent, well-to-do professional family of English and Scottish origins, the youngest of four children of Dr. Eli Kirk Crothers and Dr. Marie Depew Crothers of Bloomington, Illinois. By the time Rachel was born, the Crothers were established residents of this small but flourishing semirural midwest community. Her father had come as a boy to Illinois from Ohio and set up his medical practice in 1850. President Lincoln appointed him medical examiner of Civil War soldiers in his area, and Dr. Crothers broadened his financial resources through various business ventures, including the ownership of the largest drugstore in Bloomington.[1]

Dr. Marie Crothers, whose father was a close friend of Lincoln, came from a family of prosperous merchants and Whig organizers. After some years of assisting her husband informally, she began her medical career late in life, almost coinciding with the birth of her youngest child, Rachel. In 1877–1878 she took her first medical course at the Woman's Medical College of Pennsylvania. Two years later, Dr. Crothers returned to her medical studies in Chicago at the Woman's Medical College, and then was admitted to a gynecological course at Rush Medical College, by special intercession of influential friends. Finally, in 1882–1893, she returned to Philadelphia to complete her training and receive her Doctor of Medicine Degree.[2] Upon her return to Bloomington, Dr. Crothers set up her own medical practice, and the official records noted that she "met with a good deal of opposition, even from the profession, they not taking very kindly to the idea of women entering the profession."[3]

Dr. Marie Crothers's career brought a permanent influence to bear on the life and writings of her youngest daughter.

15

Crothers's plays are filled with strong, independent, talented women, while she herself attained high status in her profession and remained an independent woman, as did her older sister. Crothers's plays also record the independent woman's conflicting professional and domestic concerns, and one of Crothers's most important plays, *He and She,* pits a daughter's need for maternal care against her mother's passionate desire to fulfill her artistic ambitions. Clearly, once Dr. Crothers had begun her medical career, she ceased to be a full-time domestic figure. At least two reports suggest that Crothers was sent to live with an aunt in Wellesley, Massachusetts, during Dr. Crothers's student years.[4] One interviewer assumed that Crothers had always been a "lonely child" because of her mother's medical career.[5]

Except for the oddity of having two doctors as parents, then, Crothers's childhood resembled in externals that of other children comfortably born into respected families. She attended the Illinois State Normal University Grammar School, in the city of Normal, which was eventually to become linked with Bloomington; and graduated from the Illinois State Normal University High School in 1891.[6] Although she took a classical course, the driving force during her academic years was not her studies but her love for theater. Writing and producing childhood melodramas, acting with the Bloomington Dramatic Club, and leading her Sunday School pupils in educational dramatic sketches are memories which Crothers elaborates on in later writings.[7]

Crothers's early graduation from high school at age thirteen must have caused her family some concern as they cast about for an appropriate follow-up. She enrolled the next year in the New England School of Dramatic Instruction in Boston for one term, graduating in February of 1892 with a certificate from her principal, Henry Mader Pitt, testifying to her abilities as "teacher, reader, and reciter."[8] Before and after her graduation, Crothers gave what were known as "elocution recitals" in her home-town area and in Boston. Programs from these recitals announce her presentation of such works as the balcony scene from *Romeo and Juliet,* Brander Matthews's skit, "The Silent System," "The Elf Child," by James Whitcomb Riley, and excerpts from Sheridan's *The School for Scandal.*[9] Crothers's appetite for theater obviously was not satiated by her Boston training. In at least one interview of the era she announced that her intent was "ultimately to devote her talents to the dramatic art,"[10] and she yearned to go to New York to begin her career. Her family, however, refused to consent to such a plan,[11] and the aspiring actress returned to Bloomington for several years, nurturing her desire to be at the center of American theater.

Some time during 1896-1897 Crothers moved to New York and made the Metropolitan East Coast her home for the better part of her life. Two factors may have some bearing on Crothers's departure for New York during this period. First, Crothers's father died in 1893, and if he had disapproved of his daughter's goals, his death may have removed one barrier; second, Crothers turned sixteen in 1896, and that may have been the age after which she achieved sufficient maturity in her family's eyes to leave for the big city. Although some stories and press releases contradict each other regarding Crothers's move East, Crothers herself asserted that she came to New York without any paths being smoothed before her: "I knew *no one* in New York—either in or out of the theater—but I had heard of David Belasco and Daniel Frohman—and they were good enough to answer my letters and see me. But they didn't find anything in me of any value whatsoever and no jobs were forthcoming. So I decided to put my remaining and rapidly melting dollars into a short course in a school of acting. Not that I thought I needed it at all—but it would keep me in New York. I couldn't turn back. I had burned my bridges."[12]

Crothers enrolled in the Stanhope-Wheatcroft school of acting for one term as a student and remained as a teacher for at least four years, during which time she coached students, and eventually began writing and directing one-act plays which the students used to display their talents. In the fall of 1897 she made her New York acting debut with E. H. Sothern's company, and she continued to pursue a professional acting career for several seasons, appearing with the Lyceum Stock Company in New York, and a touring company of *The Christian*.[13] Between 1899 and 1903, when her one-acts began to attract notice, Crothers was making the transition from the role of supporting actress to the more difficult role of dramatist. From Crothers's perspective, the years at the drama school were exceedingly fruitful. In addition to having the opportunity to see her plays on stage, she took charge of all aspects of producing them, coaching the actors, designing the sets, costumes, and props; she regarded it as "an experience of inestimable value because the doors of the theater are very tightly closed to women in the work of directing and staging plays."[14] Although the student work was merely a rehearsal of Crothers's "tremendous ambition" to make her mark in the theater, she committed herself to it wholeheartedly, and later admitted that "there are mental records that my brain still stores, of hours and hours spent on simple details that might have been overlooked, for after all, the matinee performances were only intended to show progress of pupils."[15]

Whatever bridges Crothers humorously suggested she had burned by committing herself to the theater, they were neither social nor familial. At least, not permanently so. The social columns of Bloomington's *Daily Pantagraph* regularly reported visits between Crothers and her sister and mother, and informed the local population of advances in the career of their celebrated native daughter. Further, from a rather early point in her career, Crothers maintained a Park Avenue address, was linked by membership in various women's clubs to a well-to-do social strata, and performed within a theatrical context the type of charity work which had distinguished generations of phil-anthropic, well-born ladies: organizing holidays and entertain-ments for working girls, aiding the war effort through two world wars, and leading relief work during the Depression.[16]

From this perspective, Crothers's commitment to the theater was not so much a rejection of her family's upper-middle-class respectability, or the desire to embrace a Bohemian life-style. Rather, it was a transplanting of her family's ethical concerns and devotion to the strenuous life from the rural Midwest to the competitive soil of the American theater in New York.

II   *Apprentice Plays—1899–1905*

Crothers began her training as a dramatist and director at the beginning of the struggle to make an American drama, when efforts were barely underway to establish the respectability and financial solvency of the profession of playwright, and when New York was just becoming the capital of theater in America.[17] Although modern American drama eventually proved itself open to as many European influences as the country itself absorbed in the decades between 1890–1920, early twentieth-century American drama was heavily indebted to the nineteenth-century legacies of domestic melodrama and historical romance, written in the diction and rhythms of pseudo-Shakespearean blank verse, and acted in a highly stylized manner. Crothers's description of her childhood drama, *Every Cloud Has a Silver Lining, or The Ruined Merchant,* is almost a parody of traditional melodrama. The play's villain "carried a wooden sword, wore a black velvet cape, riding boots and red flannel underdrawers by way of doublet and hose" and the five acts alternated between forest and castle until "Happiness at Last" consumed the players in Act Five.[18]

Nevertheless, the social-problem drama, with its frank themes, its colloquial rhythms and diction, its rejection of nineteenth-century devices such as asides and tableaux, and its quieter style of acting, reflected in such rare nineteenth-century American playwrights as James Herne, stirred the imagination of many Americans, including the young Crothers, who suggested to her Bloomington dramatic society that they mount a production of Ibsen's *A Doll's House.*[19] Between 1899–1905, Crothers's apprentice plays reflect not only the forces of the commercial American theater of her time, but also the advance current of American drama, inspired by the European movement as well as by the challenge to create an authentically American drama.

Crothers's earliest plays, the one-acts written for the drama students' showcase productions, were staged at the older, second-class New York theaters.[20] *Criss-Cross, Elizabeth,* and *Mrs. John Hobbs* were seen at the Madison Square Theater in 1899;[21] *The Rector* in 1902 and *Nora* in 1903 at the Savoy Theater; and *The Point of View* in 1904 at the Manhattan Theater.[22] Crothers collaborated with Louise Morgan Sill on a five-act drama based on Hamlin Garland's novel *The Captain of the Gray Horse Troop* (1903), but it was not produced. Three of the performed one-acts exist in typescript or published form, and they constitute examples not only of Crothers's earliest works but of specific values characteristic of the American stage. The focus of dramatic attention, appropriately for showcases of student talent as well as for an era wedded to the "star" system, is Crothers's central woman character.

Criss-Cross (1899), the earliest of the produced one-acts, presents contrasting versions of feminine character at the turn of the century. The play is set in the New York apartment of Ann Chadwick, a talented and strong-minded young writer, and her cousin Cecil, a frivolous, sentimental young woman dependent upon Ann as head of this very small household. Ann is carrying out the death-bed wish of her father who, in his lifetime having always protected his younger brother, wills to Ann the duty of protecting his brother's child. Two portraits of the brothers dominate the setting and remind us throughout the act of Ann's inherited duty.

Ann's primary responsibility is to secure Cecil's marriage to a young suitor, the artist Jack Allister, whose attentions appear to be mysteriously wavering. When Ann recognizes that Jack is in love with her, and that she loves him in return, she must struggle to suppress her emotions and to give priority to her responsibilities as protector. In a very economical way, then, Crothers conveys the tension surrounding Ann's characterization as a New Woman, that is, her difficulties in inhabiting the "mixed spheres" of masculine and feminine in an age that was still dominated by separate spheres. Both Cecil and Jack see Ann's strength of character, her talent, and her self-sufficiency in a negative light, as a failure of femininity. For example, Cecil suddenly stops herself from pouring out her disappointment in her stalled romance with Jack, and ironically accuses Ann of being unable to empathize: "You're so strong and sure of things . . . you've never loved anyone. I can see you throwing him over without a pang, because of an idea" (5). And Jack, always grateful for Ann's perceptive criticism of his paintings, nevertheless criticizes her for being all "brain" and "nerves," although later he is surprised to discover "sweetness" in addition to her intellect (8).

What captures our interest in this short drama is the character of Ann, an early representative of Crothers's New-Woman figure. Since Ann has advised Cecil to regain Jack's attention through her beauty and her ability to flatter him and make him feel important, she obviously recognizes traditional feminine behavior. But the play calls our attention to the signs that Ann has rejected aspects associated with femininity: she does not concern herself with elaborate dress or toilet; she speaks her mind frankly; she acts in a brisk and confident manner; she emphasizes the strength and straightforwardness of her personality. Cecil and Jack's critical perceptions of Ann's character, then, echo their society's judgment of the New Woman as hard and rational. New Women like Ann, who displayed such masculine qualities, were presumed deficient in feminine qualities, lacking tender emotions or interest in relations with men. What Crothers demonstrates through this little play is that the social judgment of Ann is wrong. She is strong and talented, but she is also compassionate and vulnerable to romantic love. Crothers, however, avoids a direct exposition of the social conflict surrounding the problems of the New Woman and romance. She concentrates, instead, on the melodrama of hidden love, and the sacrifice of happiness to a higher duty.

In *The Rector* (1902), Crothers is once again interested in pursuing the problems of her strong and straightforward woman, but in this one-act she attempts a more complicated venture. She expands her stage characters from three to seven; conducts scenes and speeches involving more than two people; interweaves the social context more neatly into the conflict of the drama; and observes at greater length the noble renunciation of love of her strong central woman. Margaret Norton is portrayed as the single competent, frank, intelligent woman in a country congregation. She organizes the parsonage's business but, more important, she gives its young rector courage to follow his heart's promptings and to ignore the social disapproval which is sure to follow his courtship of the flirtatious Victoria Knox, a woman with a clouded reputation. What only the audience knows is that Margaret, secretly in love with John, had hoped to be his wife. Had she been manipulative or vengeful, she could easily have dissuaded John from seeing Victoria, but as she is good, strong, and noble, she champions a somewhat tarnished woman and loses her man.

Like Ann, Margaret stands apart from the majority of women, both the church gossips and the flashy Victoria. Margaret is "fresh," "confident," dresses simply—and is obviously superior to the provincial narrowness of her community. Even the rector assumes that Margaret must "sometimes rebel at this narrow little life and want something freer, broader, where you can use that beautiful mind of yours" (9). Although he admires her beautiful mind, he assumes it renders her superior or indifferent to love. As he tells her, "I've wondered so many times what sort of a man you will marry. I've thought of all the men I've known— and know, and among them all I can't find one worthy of you. I can't imagine a man daring to woo you—or thinking for a moment he could satisfy you or make you happy. But I want you to be happy. I hope I may see the completion of your glorious

womanhood" (16). In the era's code, "completion of womanhood" means marriage and maternity,[23] yet Crothers clearly
shows that superior women will most likely remain "incomplete"
in a world where man's dominance and woman's inferiority are
the basic underpinnings of romantic relations.

Despite the echo of Ibsen in the title of Crothers's third extant
one-act, *Nora* (1903), this portrayal of the central woman as
outsider rests less on her New-Woman qualities and more on her
profession in the theater. The low-born and uneducated actress
fights against the wealthy and powerful Raymond family to keep
her son. Her dead husband was their scapegrace young scion, and
although Nora and Dan Raymond were respectably married long
before the birth of their child, the family is convinced that Nora
can never provide an honorable upbringing for a child with such
distinguished lineage. Crothers shows that the rich have no
monopoly on morality. Only one of the Raymonds matches Nora's
courage and compassion; nevertheless, this one woman convinces Nora to relinquish the happiness she has known with her
son for the higher duty of allowing him to inherit noble family
traditions. This play, more than the other two, dwells at great
length on the melodramatic staple of the emotions of suffering
and prolongs the farewell between Nora and her child. However,
the large cast of ten permitted Crothers to exercise her skill at
characterization by requiring not only age and personality
distinctions, but class distinctions as well.

These three one-acts not only anticipate Crothers's dramatic
interest in women's destiny but they share qualities of the
mainstream American drama of the late nineteenth and early
twentieth centuries. Basically, the genre of serious melodrama in
which Crothers engaged was devoid both of gaiety and of satire.
The humor that exists resides in isolated exaggerations of
character foibles, or buffoonish behavior. In addition to the
melodramatic tableau and monologue noted in *Criss Cross,* and
the tearful farewell in *Nora, The Rector* has a roll-call entrance
of individual characters who, by means of asides, mimed actions,
and exaggerated expressions, reveal necessary background
information to the audience, forward the narrative, and directly
comment to the audience on other characters and actions. As in
most nineteenth-century American drama, complication comes
from plotted events and not from personality or motivation.
Some dramatic techniques, however, are clearly influenced by

modern realistic drama. Although Crothers's results are amateurish, she does attempt to bury her exposition of past events within the forward action of the play. She is most successful in *Criss-Cross*, where the history of the fateful death-bed promise is necessary to understand Ann's actions and is foreshadowed by the portraits and told at an appropriate time. She is least successful in *Nora*, when the Raymond family members discuss among themselves those past events which have shaped the present and which are, obviously, well-known enough to the family so that they are recounted purely for the edification of the audience. And Crothers's dramatic characterization certainly reflects woman's changing status. The fate of her three strong women, to suffer their loneliness, deprived of the men (or boy) they love, is both a direct function of their strength and an indirect reflection of Crothers's social thesis regarding the unjust treatment of the New Woman.

III *First Success*

Crothers entered the arena of professional playwriting in 1906 after several years of frustration. The economic conditions of the American theater in the early years of the twentieth century, although better for playwrights than the old stock system,[24] produced among them fierce competition to forge successful careers. Leading actors or actresses often commissioned plays, but hopeful dramatists regularly sent them unsolicited manuscripts, especially tailored to the qualities of the star.[25] There were also playwriting studios in which many a would-be dramatist labored, reworking another author's play for production until he could place his own.[26] Although the turn-of-the-century American theater had produced at least four millionaire playwrights and had provided careers between 1870 and 1910 for several dramatists of substance,[27] nevertheless the hurdles were very high for the newcomer.

The commercial manager was the dominant economic force in the American theater, but by 1896 there arose an even more powerful influence, the theatrical trust begun by businessmen A. L. Erlanger and Marc Klaw.[28] Joined by other theater owners, and by the producer Charles Frohman, they formed a syndicate ostensibly to eliminate competition but actually to gain control of most of the important theaters in the metropolitan cities and almost all of the theaters in outlying towns whose one-night stands provided crucial economic links for plays touring the metropolitan areas. By controlling the theaters, the Syndicate could also control the managers, the players, and, ultimately, the playwrights, who feared they would be cut off from their audiences, particularly by being closed out of first-class houses. The Syndicate never completely ruled the American theater, Mrs. Fiske holding out during the fiercest early years of the struggle, Bernhardt playing in a tent when Syndicate theaters were closed to her. Further, their control was shortlived, since by 1905 the Shubert brothers had broken the trust's monopoly. Nevertheless, although it is difficult to measure precisely the Syndicate's influence on American drama, its preferences clearly had to affect the playwright fighting for a toe-hold in the theater.[29] It admired plays that attracted the widest possible audience, avoided the dullness of "austere or tragic" drama such as that of the modern European dramatists, and emphasized "entertainment" and "diversion from care."[30] Such values dominated one portion of the commercial theater for decades.

Crothers seems to have consciously avoided the Syndicate with the successful production of her first professional piece, *The Three of Us* (1906), at the independently owned Madison Square Theater. It ran for 227 performances and in the following year it was transferred to London with Ethel Barrymore as star and with Crothers supervising the production.[31] The play bears marks of Crothers's growing confidence in her craft, and of her interest in the New Woman. In Eaton's overview of the first years of twentieth-century American drama, he cites it as one sign of growth in the American theater.[32] It does not, however, break away from the prevailing criteria of theatrical success, shared by Syndicate and independent theater managers alike, to say nothing of the vast majority of America's playwrights.

Set in a Nevada mining town, the play is a domestic melodrama in four acts, and alternates between the comic and serious modes, just as its characters' fortunes fluctuate between triumph and defeat. What dominates the play is a complicated series of intrigues surrounding the ownership of a silver mine, stark contrasts between good and bad characters who fight for control of the mine, and a romantic reconciliation of the play's lovers— the staples of popular drama. Nevertheless, the play's concern with a social theme, although minor, indicates the direction in which Crothers was heading.

The play has a large case of characters, but focuses on a family of three orphans, a young woman and her two younger brothers, who have inherited a barren silver mine and their father's dying wish that they stick together. Their unity is threatened, however, by the hardships of poverty and the temptations of wealth. The central figure in this household, and head of it for the past decade since her parents' death, is twenty-five-year-old Rhy MacChesney. Unlike her discontented brother, Clem, Rhy does not suffer from their lack of wealth or material comfort, nor does she exhibit any of the traditional weaknesses associated with her sex. Both her poverty and her femininity, however, render her extremely vulnerable, in characteristic melodramatic fashion, to the villain who stalks through the play as a representative of unscrupulous wealth. But what lifts the action above the level of melodramatic cliché is that the conflict over woman's honor between Rhy and the villain is repeated in the conflict between Rhy and her upright suitor. Both men are guilty of demeaning women through the imposition of the dual moral standard, and although Crothers delivers no direct criticism of the social bases of the code, she does show its cruelty, whether imposed by good men or bad.

Rhy's physical appearance, described in stage directions and emphasized by her first actions on stage, indicates that Crothers intended her to represent the New Woman, at least in part. On her entrance, Rhy drags in a heavy trunk; she then drops down on her knees, catches keys "like a boy," and shouts out a variety of orders to everyone in sight, a clear contrast to the usually elegant entrance of the lady star. As Crothers describes her, Rhy is "forceful and fearless as a young Amazon, with the courage of belief in herself—the audacity and innocence of youth which has never known anything but freedom—. . . . What she wears is very far from the fashion but has charm and individuality and leaves her free and unconscious of her strength and beauty as an animal" (11). Rhy is no comic reversal of the traditionally helpless woman, such as Howard's tomboy, Jenny Buckthorn, in *Shenandoah.* Nor are the New-Woman qualities the dominating aspect of her personality. Although Rhy may avoid frills and fluttery behavior, no one mistakes her strength for indifference to romance. She has no difficulty attracting propositions or proposals, and we see in her characterization Crothers's attempt to overcome the disabilities of her earlier heroines, who were always disappointed in love.

The plot of the play is built on a growing number of secrets, a legacy of the nineteenth-century well-made play. The secrets serve to increase the tension and complication of the action, and have a thematic function as well, since secrets and woman's honor become intertwined. The first secret is that Townley, Rhy's honest suitor, has discovered a magnificent vein of ore running through the adjacent silver mines owned by Rhy, the neighboring Bix family, and himself. Realizing that they have neither the individual nor the collective means to extract the silver, Townley prepares to interest a syndicate man. When he shares the news with Rhy, he swears her to secrecy until he can make a solid deal, and for Rhy, the fact that he has trusted her, "the rarest thing a man gives to a woman" (43), symbolizes his deepest love. Unknown to either of them, however, is that Clem has eavesdropped and, driven by poverty and anger, he sells the secret to Louis Berresford, the villainous rich man whose designs Rhy has consistently rebuffed. Berresford hastily purchases the Bix mine, pretending sympathy for the couple's desire to return to the civilized East, but requiring them to keep secret his identity as buyer. Finally, in one of the last secrets, Berresford manipulates Rhy into learning and keeping his secret by first taunting her with woman's reputation as a chatterbox.

Problems surrounding Rhy's honor mount when Trenholm, the syndicate man, discovers that the Bix mine is sold. Since only Townley and Rhy knew of the discovery, Trenholm, and Townley as well, are convinced that she has gossiped. Imprisoned in her word of honor to keep Berresford's secret, Rhy can only plead for her beloved's trust, but he denounces her as having "done the worst thing a woman can do—sold out one man for another" (64). In order to free herself from her promise, Rhy visits Berresford's home at night to plead for her "honor" and "integrity" (75). When he refuses to release her, she defies him, arguing that "honor means common sense" and refusing "to sacrifice the happiness of two people for a silly empty promise" (75).

Rhy thinks of her honor as her integrity as a person, and she objects to being trapped by the letter rather than the spirit of a code of honor. She is all the more surprised, then, when Berresford narrows the meaning of woman's honor to the state of her sexual virtue. From his point of view, her unchaperoned midnight visit to his rooms will condemn her in the eyes of society as surely as any actions she might perform. Therefore, she might just as well submit to his advances and become his mistress. Crothers has built the scene to emphasize Rhy's stunned reaction to Berresford's claim, and she refuses to submit to any arbitrary judgment on her behavior in ringing tones: "It's true then—all women must be afraid. I haven't believed it. I've thought we could do anything that was *right* in *itself.* I still think it! I *know* it! A good woman hasn't anything to be afraid of. I'm not afraid of the *world.* . . ."(79). Rhy's fearlessness is then tested when Townley bursts into Berresford's room and, seeing Rhy there, assumes the worst, just as Berresford had predicted. Now Townley insists that Rhy marry Berresford to save her honor. Enraged by the alliance of the men, she ridicules their postures as "protector," and closes the act on a declaration of independence: "My honor! Do you think it's in your hands? It's in my own and I'll take care of it, and everyone who *belongs* to me. I don't need you—either of you" (79).

Rhy's defiance, however, becomes totally reversed in the final act. Once she learns that Clem has sold the secret to Berresford, and once she recognizes that Clem's frustrations have arisen because she has "dominated" Clem as head of the household, she bends her efforts toward restoring his shaky self-image and the damaged family unit. She enlists Clem in a superior role in the family, assuring him that she needs his help and guidance, particularly now that the whole town is gossiping about her visit to Berresford. His self-respect and strength increase in direct proportion to the growth of his perception of Rhy as helpless. Even the traditionally happy ending of the lover's reconciliation seems skewed toward the effort to rehabilitate Clem. In Rhy's curtain line to Townley, she glances toward Clem and says, "We must make a good man of him. I have you to help me" (100).

Rhy emerges from this drama both as the critical, assertive New Woman who shoulders responsibilities presumably reserved for men, and as the traditional woman, yearning for love, submitting to the power of man, and, in the case of Clem, deftly pulling all the strings behind his back. Although Rhy's character undergoes a radical change between Acts Three and Four, the change seems wholly consistent with the requirements of producing a satisfactory play, a feminist heroine being clearly unacceptable to the country's audiences. Nevertheless, Crothers's portrayal is double edged: Rhy capitulates to principles she has already condemned, such as the importance of woman's honor, or woman's need of man's protection. And Crothers has underscored the pitiable weakness of Clem as well as the absurdity of the male code to which Rhy submits.

The perceptions of contemporaneous critics suggest how Crothers succeeded in making Rhy's New-Woman criticisms acceptable to her road audiences, a more conservative determiner of theatrical fare than the New York audience. The *Toledo Blade,* for example, saw Rhy's turning to her brother for support as a "masterstroke" of womanly intuition that could only have been conceived by a woman playwright. The play is praised as a true mirror of society because it reflects one of life's realities, "that women accomplish only by being 'diplomatic' with his 'egotistical highness, man' " and by keeping the "secret of her success to herself."[33] And a Chicago critic noted approvingly that, at the play's end, Rhy's "sphere is narrowed down to a sister's helpfulness with her view smilingly fixed upon a wedding ring" and expressed relief that her character is not "the emancipating trumpeter of noisy deeds for femininity, but the holy woman of the great resplendent life of throbbing motherhood."[34] Certainly, from this perspective, we must be wary of oversimplifying Rhy as an "outstanding representative of the new woman,"[35] or the play as "the first of a series of plays in which Miss Crothers went forth to champion her sex, to decry the double standard of morality by which men and women were judged."[36] Crothers certainly betrays a concern for the social fate of women, but by fashioning a successful play, she tells us more about the limits on the portrayal of the New-Woman character than she tells us about the concerns of the American New Woman in the first decade of the twentieth century.

Generally, critical reception of the play was enthusiastic, praising Crothers's naturalistic details of setting and speech, the attractive characterization of Rhy, and the originality of her denunciation of both men. Those critics who commented negatively on parts of the play criticized its "parochial ideas"[37] and the stereotyped characterization of Berresford, whom Eaton called "the inevitable woman's villain who never drew breath of life."[38] Perhaps the best insight afforded by the criticism is Eaton's recognition of Crothers's serious concerns. He predicted that in her future plays she would "bring a woman's tact and insight to bear on our vexed domestic problems."[39]

IV   *First Failure*

Crothers's great success with *The Three of Us* was followed by the equally clear failure of her next production, *The Coming of Mrs. Patrick* (1907).[40] The play closed after thirteen performances. Like the earlier success, the play is a melodrama, but more domestic than romantic, and more domesticated than adventurous. It takes place in a gloomy and disorganized New York mansion, where the lady of the house has been bed-ridden for years. The younger Lawtons and their befuddled father are presided over by the joyless eldest Lawton daughter, Ellinor, until the transforming influence of Mrs. Patrick revitalizes the entire household, although the indomitably cheerful widowed nurse has been hired only to treat the invalided mother. What motivates the plot are the various conflicts and misunderstandings that arise when Mrs. Patrick tries to arrange the romantic affairs of the family members and ultimately accepts her own romantic destiny. In addition to its emphasis on romance, the play is suffused with an aura of optimism and presents its case for a cheerful and spontaneous angel in the house as preferable to any oppressive rule, no matter how high-minded.

But while the play is definitely concerned with women, it contributes little to the issue of woman's freedom and does not explicitly champion any feminist cause. Indeed, the play seems almost to avoid any mention of a social issue even when the opportunity seems most ripe. For example, Mrs. Patrick's honor and virtue are unjustly condemned in a typical case of contrasting moral standards being applied to men and women, and the woman being convicted of immorality on the basis of appearances. Mrs. Patrick accepts the condemnation and, although she is ultimately vindicated, no one discusses the matter in the context of a larger social issue. Nevertheless, there are some women's concerns reflected in the play's themes and characterizations. The importance of woman's role in organizing a household and providing the proper intellectual and moral model is stressed at a time when suffragists were arguing that the wider household of the community had need of woman's superior management abilities and moral qualities. In the same vein of social welfare, one of the subplots concerns the fate of an attractive artist's model who was seduced and abandoned by the artist. Mrs. Patrick has helped to rehabilitate the woman in the

past, and when she crosses Mrs. Patrick's path again, the nurse
saves her from a soul-destroying adventure and helps set her up
as a respectable seamstress with her own shop. Thus, beneath
this solid domestic melodrama are the buds of social problems,
not simply conflicts between good and evil, and uneasily fused in
the characterization of Mrs. Patrick is another image of a New
Woman, professional, powerful, and completely charming.

Its failure made a lasting impression on the young playwright.
Two decades later Crothers recalled that, although many
managers had rejected the play, no one identified its problems
until playwright James Forbes criticized the entanglements of
the plot. His suggestion was to "cut out all this other stuff and
stick to the main story,"[41] advice Crothers wished she had taken,
for she had to agree with the critics who condemned the play for
its "old ghosts of make believe and plot and invention," whereas,
by contrast, *The Three of Us* was a "straightforward" story. [42]

Explaining the failures, as well as the successes, is always risky,
but the contemporary reader might disagree that the intrigues
surrounding the silver mines and Rhy's reputation constitute a
"straightforward story," except in contrast to the unsuccessful
play. The story line in *The Coming of Mrs. Patrick* is almost lost in
a tangle of four simultaneously unraveling subplots, and the
questions surrounding Mrs. Patrick's motives and honor involve
at least two of the play's three love triangles. Thus, the strength
of a single line of tension to secure the audience's attention is
diminished. The play even glosses over its heroine's triumphant
victory, focusing its climax of attention instead on the patient
whom she has helped to recovery.

In addition to its weaknesses of plot and structure, the play is
weaker in its characterization than the former play, particularly
in the character of Mrs. Patrick, which is never clearly
communicated to the audience. Crothers presents both a "free
spirit" and a disciplined professional; a lady with a somewhat
cloudy past, whose sufferings have made her sensitive to the
needs of others, and one who is incapable of recognizing when a
man is in love with her, and not with another woman; a romantic
soul who believes that young people should marry only for love,
and a snob who condemns marriage between members of
different social classes. Further, Mrs. Patrick is so full of energy,
and so much into everyone else's business, that the multiple
display of her talents becomes both tiresome and comic, while

her central talent as nurse is ignored. Nevertheless, the critic of *Theater* saw in the play the kind of "freedom from conventionality" and "newness of subject and character" which bode well for a theater hoping to banish stock characters.[43]

CHAPTER 2

The Social Problem Playwright
Begins to Emerge

I An American Focus on Social Problems

CROTHERS began to build her professional reputation before the end of the first decade of the new century, not by turning out agreeable farces, romance adventures, or adaptations of historical novels, but by elaborating on the social themes which had been implicit in the plots and characterizations of her earlier plays. In the apprentice plays, the portrayal of environmental forces in woman's life was largely restricted to details of decor and setting; in her development as a social-problem playwright, Crothers paid greater attention to the environment of ideas, to the force of the intellectual climate inhabited by her dramatic figures. Crothers avoided the strict determinism of naturalist playwrights, but as she considered the motives behind the behavior of her women characters, the influence of currents in the world became more important than personal whims.

Several Crothers characters from this era clash with the norms of their environment and propose theories or ideologies which attempt to change people or change society. Although the society which Crothers exposes is not always as unjust as some of her more radical characters claim, nevertheless, this is the most revolutionary phase of her dramatic career. Critics have mocked the American dramatic revolt as a mild tremor in comparison with the shocking vibrations already sent out by advanced European drama, or with the waves made by American novelists, but, as Krutch points out, there were crucial differences in theatrical conditions between the Old and New World. Audiences and dramatists in America during this era shared common convictions, whereas Ibsen and Shaw held views that were
32

radically incompatible with those of their middle-class audiences. By distinguishing between the "intellectual pioneering" of Ibsen and Shaw and the "theatrical" pioneering of "the first Americans to exploit the dramatic possibilities of certain aspects of modern life and modern attitudes,"[1] Krutch describes early modern American drama in terms relevant to the American, rather than the European, theatrical context.

II New Woman in a Hostile, Old Setting

Myself Bettina (1908) was the first play in which Crothers showed her deepening commitment to social problem drama. The play was a commercial and critical failure, surviving only thirty-two performances at Daly's Theater and attracting severely negative criticism for the first time in Crothers's development. Nevertheless the play is something of a milestone in Crothers's career. Her detailed social milieu shows the influence of modern European naturalist drama, while the story line, as critics of the play overemphasized, resembled Sudermann's *Magda*, a rather heavy late-nineteenth-century domestic tragedy on the theme of woman's honor. Maxine Elliott, the star to whom she had sold the play, gave Crothers her first professional opportunity to stage and direct a play. As Crothers put it, the commercially astute actress had "such an admiration for and faith in the work of women, that she was delighted to find a woman who could shoulder the entire responsibility."[2]

The play is a four-act domestic drama with a romantic center. It follows the conflicts encountered by a young woman, Bettina Dean, on her return to the small New England town of her birth after experiencing the revolutionary moral and intellectual freedom of Europe. Bettina attempts to promote the cause of personal freedom and to live as a model of it, but she is thwarted in both attempts by her conservative, puritanical town, and by her romantic attachment to a young clergyman. Thus, where the romantic complications in *The Coming of Mrs. Patrick* arise solely from the devices of melodrama—misunderstandings, unnoticed cues of love, and triangles—the romantic conflicts in *Myself Bettina* reflect opposing ideologies regarding women's status. Perhaps most importantly, the play's subplot enhances the theme of barriers to freedom rather than distracting from it as did the previous play's welter of plot strands. Crothers focuses

on a woman who in fact, rather than in appearance, has broken
the double moral standard and stands to lose her freedom
because of it. The play, however, is not overwhelmingly serious
or rational. Indeed, it would be more accurate to say that
Crothers has devoted perhaps half the play to her social theses,
and that she enlivens the drama's other half by music and
spectacle.

As the central character, and the first of Crothers's New
Women to be young, fashionable, alluring, and assertive, Bettina
commands our attention for almost the entire play. Her parents
dead, one of the most crucial features of her life has been
economic independence, made possible by a small inheritance
from her mother. With this money, Bettina has financed four
years in Europe training for an operatic career. A second
important feature is that Bettina takes up residence with the
Marshall family, close friends of the late elder Deans, and joins
her half sister, Mamie, who has lived there during Bettina's
absence.

Crothers charts the conflict between Bettina and her sur-
roundings from the moment the play begins. The curtain rises on
the Marshall home, with Christine Marshall, the stern maiden
sister, presiding over the ritual cleaning of the house. The chaos
of rolled-up rugs and disarranged furniture becomes organized
under Christine's rule, and we see very quickly, as the
candlesticks must "go" in their specified places on the mantel,
for example, that tradition has rigidified into a straitjacket. When
Bettina arrives, breathless and high spirited, she flings her
belongings about in defiance of the hypercleanliness and order in
the house, immediately arousing Christine's opposition. Although
Christine represents the ideal religious woman, Crothers portrays her as a thoroughly unpleasant person. She carries
patriarchal admonitions against the "worldly" woman to such an
extreme that the religious philosophy she upholds is also
negatively framed.

Opposition to Bettina is portrayed more ambiguously,
however, in the character of John Marshall, the youngest in the
long line of Marshall ministers. John is personally and
philosophically more attractive than Christine; he had also been
Bettina's beau before she left for Europe, and is now engaged to
Mamie. Crothers emphasizes John as a representative of the new
social conscience of Christianity. His clear links to the puritanical
prohibitions of his religion, however, serve to implicate him

more subtly than Christine in the oppression of woman's freedom. He opposes most of Bettina's attempts to spread her gospel of freedom to the townspeople—such as her desire to present Oscar Wilde's erotic *Salomé* at a church social—as immature and trivial. On another occasion, he opposes Bettina's desire to go to a public dance in a neighboring town. John claims he is neither a prude nor a puritan, but a realist. Shocking his community for aesthetic or abstract reasons would jeopardize his mission: to jostle the townspeople into providing better conditions for the town's poor and into supporting a program for rehabilitating criminals within the community. Bettina denounces John as a hypocrite, but set against his earnest reform efforts, Bettina's complaints against restrictive moral codes are made to seem petty and self-indulgent.

The ideological conflicts between Bettina and John both heighten and reflect their romantic relationship. He clearly rebuffs her attempts to rekindle their romance when the play begins, but during the course of the play, Crothers makes us aware of John's gradually reviving interest in Bettina. His disapproval of Bettina's ideas, however, hinders their reunion. In the quarrel between Bettina and John over the prospects of freedom for the town, the contest ultimately reduces to one between the demands of "self" and the responsibilities of "duty," an argument familiar to prewar audiences who were conscious of women's issues.[3] From John's perspective, Bettina is not so much at war with society as she is at war with herself. When he claims that her "older, better self" is at war with her "new, selfish self," his rhetoric echoes the charges of selfishness against the New Woman.

In the play's subplot, however, Bettina's New-Woman ideology prevails, and Bettina herself learns how strongly she, too, has been influenced by oppressive codes for women. The subplot concerns the love affair between Lennox, the callow younger Marshall brother, and Mamie, the latter hiding her anguish behind a façade of domestic, contented womanhood. Crothers portrays Mamie as a victim not just of Lennox's smooth manners and seductive promises but of the repressive atmosphere of household and town, which prohibits her enjoyment of life and youth except in illicit ways. Thus, she is hurt by John's best intentions as well as by Lennox's worst ones. At the most abstract level, Mamie is a victim of contrasting moral standards for the sexes, an attitude held by even the most apparently worldly of women. When Bettina carelessly flirts with Lennox, Mamie is propelled by fear of losing the man into revealing her indiscretion to her sister. The tongue-lashing she receives from her emphasizes how ingrained are the prejudices against the sexually active woman. For Bettina, Mamie's plight is disgraceful, degrading, and "the one thing in this world a woman can not excuse" (III, 2). Only when Christine mistakenly judges Bettina guilty of immoral actions and holds her accountable to this rigid judgment does the young woman recognize the injustice she has perpetrated on her sister.

As the subplot complications begin to unravel, and John learns of the affair, he accepts the news in a spirit of Christian forgiveness. He does not blame Mamie, but he insists that she marry Lennox in order to be made the traditionally honest woman. It is at this point, the ideological climax of the play, that Bettina's New Woman arguments, now against forced marriage and for a new definition of woman's honor, come into play. As Crothers presents them, they are more respectable than traditional Christianity, and more advanced than the reforms to which John dedicates his life.

Bettina has called John's values "cramped," "strait-laced," "old-fashioned" and the antithesis to life itself. She accuses the Marshall household, and the traditions it upholds and reflects, of being the cause of Mamie's wrongdoings and, therefore, incompetent to judge or punish her. Bettina abhors any social, theological, or economic considerations that enter into marriage, arguing that love alone should motivate the union between women and men. Forced marriage becomes a hypocritical façade of decency which would make Mamie neither respectable nor happy. The way for Mamie to recover dignity and her woman's honor as a person, according to this philosophy, is by dint of her own hard work, increasing the dormant talents and skills that have been stifled during her domestic years in the Marshall home. In short, she must feel worthy as a person in her own right, and not as an adjunct to a man. In order to aid Mamie in this effort, Bettina transfers to her her mother's inheritance so that she can go to Europe and study voice, a clear break with the repressive community, and a clear recapitulation of Bettina's career.

Bettina's arguments ultimately persuade John that the marriage must be called off and that Mamie must have her chance in the world. The philosophy of freedom prevails over the "old-fashioned" values. Nevertheless. the play is not a clear championing of the liberated woman. When Bettina transfers her money to Mamie, she reverses her own fortunes, but, far from becoming an economic dependent in the Marshall household and repeating her sister's sad story, she catalyzes her romantic reunion with John. John terms her gesture a "miracle" of unselfish love, pronounces Bettina returned to her old self, and the "new" self, the promoter of individual rights, dissolves into a charming, sweet, submissive woman, an appropriate partner for marriage.

In evaluating the play as a whole, its greatest weaknesses arise from Bettina's sudden reversal. Although the play exposes a hostile social and theological climate to woman, and blames the vindictiveness of some aspects of Christian practice, it blunts its indictment of this environment. Ultimately, the play splits its original premise: it argues that the chances for independent woman's integrity and success are slim in an environment which is emotionally and theologically hostile to both, and it slips into the comfortable dramatic niche that ignores woman's integrity and confines success to marriage. Crothers is concerned with issues of economic independence and social justice for women, but she buries these beneath her concern to secure romance and marriage for her New Woman. The play's characterization is weakened as the two sisters exchange dominant qualities in the final scenes; and, in terms of dramatic craftsmanship, the structure of the play is badly marred by the most wearisome device. The two critical confrontations of the play take place only because Mamie has twice hidden behind curtains and has overheard important exchanges which then lead to confessions.

What we judge as failures, however, are the conventions of success that dominated the theater in Crothers's day. In an attempt to avoid conflict with a mass audience, Bettina's character ultimately conforms to what the critics had praised in Crothers's previous women characters: traditional womanly qualities and goals. Bettina casts aside feminism to secure marriage, devoid, for the first time in the play, of any critical insights into her situation. Despite these manipulations, the major impression she left in the critics' minds was a negative one.

Bettina, they claimed, was too selfish a heroine to be sympathetic.[4]

Critics also lacked sympathy with Crothers's aspirations as a
social dramatist, as well as with her drama. In Burns Mantle's
review in the *Chicago Tribune* (Feb. 13, 1908) he called the play
"a modest little comedy drama in which the theme is so much
more impressive than the manner of its handling that it creates
the impression of being topheavy. . . . Miss Crothers is
thoroughly earnest and no doubt feels more deeply on the
subject she introduces than she is able to express, but she has
invaded a field in which the German and Norwegian masters of
the psychological drama have preceded her and her efforts are
bound to appear trivial in comparison with theirs."[5]

But as the first of Crothers's social-problem dramas, the play
shows clear advances. The plot structure is more compact and
condensed than in previous plays, showing a marked awareness
of certain European tendencies such as the late point of attack,
the more subtle interweaving of exposition with the forward
action, the selection of entirely ordinary events, rather than
adventure, to aid the impression of reality, and the single
building toward a high point of action and reversal, rather than
the see-saw action of melodrama where characters are on the
brink of triumph or disaster until the last moment of the play.
Although the defects in the play are great, in theme, characterization, and dramatic form, Crothers entered *Myself Bettina*
as a "trial" serious drama and discovered the pitfalls as well as
the challenges of such an enterprise.

III *Fighting the Androcentric Culture:* A Man's World

Crothers followed the advance currents of the social-problem
drama with her next play, *A Man's World* (1909), in which she
depicts the struggles of a young woman novelist, Frank Ware, to
maintain her ideals in woman's freedom and her work for
woman's progress. Crothers also explores the effect of the past
on the relationship between Frank and the man she hopes to
marry. When Frank discovers his indifference to fathering an
illegitimate child, she dissolves their relationship. Flexner
praised the drama for tackling "the question of the double
standard more unequivocally and intelligently than it had yet

been treated by an American dramatist."[6] This praise, however, narrows the scope of the playwright's attack, just as the brief plot summary above, which formed the basis of critical judgments, reduces Frank's feminist beliefs to a singularly punitive philosophy. In fact, Crothers condemns the double standard as just one of the symptoms of a larger cultural malaise stemming from the androcentric culture, the man's world of the title.

The play was not a commercial success, with only seventy-one performances at New York's Comedy Theater. It did, however, provoke debate and argument in newspapers and journals, indicating at least the critical interest in mainstream American theater's coming of age. Eaton noted the play's "obvious significance as a comment on the feminist movement of the day,"[7] and it seems likely that Crothers consciously disregarded the criterion of "satisfying amusement." Her sympathetic portrayal of an active feminist, and her uncompromising thematic insistence on a single standard of sexual morality, both qualities necessary to express her dramatic vision, were unlikely to capture a wide audience. Crothers hesitated, however, to divorce herself publicly from the realm of entertainment. "The playwright's province," she claimed, "is not reform," and she refuted any intention to "preach," content instead to clothe her convictions "in a dramatic story and make an entertaining play."[8] Nevertheless, Crothers did not hesitate to declare that she shared the convictions and principles of her feminist character.

Frank's conflicts with the imperatives of male power provide Crothers the opportunity to condemn some of the more deeply entrenched social injustices of her time. And though she concentrates on those injustices to women, Frank's reforming zeal reflects the larger social context of the play, the social-reform movement in America. Women played a dominant role in the settlement-house movement, working-girls' clubs, improved housing and sanitation in the slums, battles against prostitution and for prostitutes' rehabilitation. Against this particular background, we recognize the legitimacy of Frank's work and ideals: her belief in the validity of the life of the independent woman; and her desire to reverse the social decay which she believed resulted from the immorality, not just of individual men, but of the code which sanctioned their behavior.

Crothers sets her play in a New York boardinghouse populated by male and female artists, a modern environment for her liberated woman, and a convenient domestic setting which facilitates the comings and goings of a variety of people. Crothers's Bohemians accept a freer life-style and hold more advanced views on some subjects but, with the exception of Frank, they have conservative attitudes toward woman's abilities and status. In their convictions that there must be practical limits to the theory of woman's freedom and talents, they mirror the mainstream society. Frank lives in the house with her adopted son, Kiddie, and earns her living as a writer. She considers herself a "free" and "natural" woman, with no constraints on her behavior, but she clearly arouses the suspicions and prejudices of those around her.

When the play begins, Frank's latest novel, a sociological documentary of the Lower East Side ghetto, *The Beaten Path*, has been highly praised by the critics, but in terms patronizing to woman's talent. One review notes that when Frank's first work attracted wide attention, it was thought she was a man, "but now that we know she is a woman we are more than ever impressed by the strength and scope of her work. . ." (11). Although Frank's friends are pleased by her success, they suspect it was due to a man's help rather than to her talent. One antagonist in the house, a jealous woman singer, goes even further by suggesting that Frank is merely posing as a "strong minded" and "independent" woman in order to hide her romance with another roomer, the newspaperman Malcolm Gaskell. She also raises the first doubts about Frank's virtue, intimating that Frank is probably Kiddie's real mother but is ashamed to reveal her past. In short, the prevailing attitude is that a richly talented, joyfully independent, virtuous woman is a contradiction to all the accepted limitations on woman's nature.

Frank is both admired and attacked for being a superior woman, and Crothers establishes her uniqueness as a heroine in a number of ways. In the opening scenes, for example, Kiddie is being amused by several of Frank's male friends until she returns from work. Upon her arrival, the men cluster around to perform various small services: fetching her slippers, taking her gloves, settling her on the sofa, bringing dinner—services which the woman normally performs for the man. This deliberate reversal of the ordinary sex roles is carefully handled. The men are not demeaned by the service, as would have been the case had Frank been a *femme fatale,* nor is Frank rendered as a bossy shrew. The clue to how the scene should be played resides in Crothers's stage directions describing Frank on her entrance: "She smiles at them all with the frank abandon of being one of them—strong, free, unafraid, with the glowing charm of a woman at the height of her development." (18).

Another clue to Frank's distinctive character is her background, which emerges during the course of the play. Like Bettina, she has lived abroad and, by implication, avoided the cramped oppressiveness of America. She was raised by her father, a writer, to read, to think, to keep her eyes open to the realities about her, and "to touch all kinds of life" (35). Her upbringing, then, is in contrast to the coy, decorous, refined model of femininity held up for admiration by her era.

The feature that establishes Frank as a unique figure in American drama is her active involvement in the cause of woman's freedom. Frank has had an early initiation into truths that her society is invested in disguising, and most particularly she has learned that "women had the worst of it" in a world where men have all the power (35). When Frank and her father were living in Paris, they befriended a frightened, unwed young American woman— Kiddie's mother—who died soon after giving birth. To the young Frank, already aware of the burden of woman's subordinate sexual status, this event was instrumental in forging her professional goals as well as increasing her personal abhorrence of relations with men. Upon Frank's return to America, she has taken up the cause of poor women, and the wretched East Side conditions which force them into prostitution, degradation, and a complete bondage to poverty. Frank has been a daily and nightly visitor to the slums, writing novels from her observations in order to expose the social crimes against these women, and helping to establish a settlement house to train, shelter, and rehabilitate these women. Frank is convinced that if the women of the ghetto had respectable work at respectable wages, they would be freed from their sexual exploitation and their bondage to men.

With this social-reform consciousness as a background to Frank's life, the play engages its central problem of freeing middle-class women from their social and sexual domination. Through Frank's romance with Malcolm Gaskell, Crothers demonstrates the more subterranean social tyranny which threatens woman's integrity. The play exposes to a critical light the arguments of necessity, law, and right, all of which have been determined by the man's world, and all of which form barriers to woman's freedom and progress.

One of the strongest barriers to woman's freedom is the doctrine that she is perpetually enthralled by sexual sins of the past and that she must be open to scrutiny for possible misdeeds in the present. Thus, gossip regarding Frank's relationship to Kiddie, and the growing demand that Frank acknowledge that she is his biological mother, represent strong forces antithetical to woman's freedom. Since Frank insists on keeping secret the real facts of Kiddie's birth from everyone except one male confidant, she increases confusion and multiplies plot complications. Crothers endows the secret with thematic integrity, however, and Frank is credible in her refusal to bow to pressure to cleanse her reputation or to elaborate on Kiddie's misfortune. But as Frank insists on her right to be judged on her present merits, she alienates most of her friends, and her philosophy makes independence a lonely experience.

What is even more crucial to the play's theme is Frank's difficulty in holding fast to this principle when pressed by the man she loves. She argues that Malcolm should accept her "just as you see me here—just as you accept a man" (72), but he replies that love prohibits equality in relations between men and women. As he sees it, when a man loves a "good" woman, he not only wants to protect and understand her, but he has the "right" to know her life. These rights accrue solely to men in love, however, not to women. When Frank asserts the similar right to have Gaskell "prove to me that everything in your life has been just what I think it ought to be" (73), Gaskell insists that his rights are inherent in his sexual identity: "I'm a man. You're a woman. I love you. I have a right to know your life" (74). Thus, romance in a society which supports masculine privileges becomes a barrier to woman's integrity and ultimately destroys her freedom. The fact that Frank, of all women, finally gives in to her love for Gaskell, makes the force of this norm even greater.

Crothers has obviously emphasized Frank's problems by bringing her into a traditional relationship with a traditional man, but the force of Gaskell's arguments is not solely a function of his "masterful" personality; he represents the extreme version of views echoed by various members of the rooming house, by the society at large. Crothers concentrates on exposing the effects of his personality and philosophy on Frank's self-image and integrity. His masculine code touches a variety of subjects and emphasizes two main judgments of woman; that her nature is emotional, submissive, and morally superior to man's; and that her behavior is subject to man's approval. Gaskell is aware that a new breed of woman, such as Frank, challenges his version of womanhood, so he trains most of his scorn on her work and ideals. He charges her book with being "too big" a task for her; he scoffs at her settlement work, and at working women in general, since in his view no matter what women do, they always remain the emotional creatures they are, incomplete without a man. "Women are only meant to be loved," he tells Frank in one of their first sparring matches, "and men have got to take care of them" (13), and he predicts she will acknowledge this truth when she falls in love. To Frank's cry of injustice to women, Gaskell answers that contrasting moral standards are a necessity: "Man sets the standard for woman. He knows she's better than he is and he demands that she be — and if she isn't, she's got to suffer for it" (40). In summary, Gaskell is adamant about his dominance: "Why this is a man's world. Women'll never change anything" (40).

By bringing their conflict to a head with the identification of Gaskell as Kiddie's father, Crothers makes the issues of the double standard an emblem of all the other issues she has raised. At first, blinded by love, Frank denies seeing any resemblance between a painted miniature of Kiddie and Malcolm. But as the gossip grows, she finally elicits from him some details of his relationship with Kiddie's mother in Paris. Gaskell readily acknowledges his affair with the woman, and although he claims he is not proud of it, neither is he ashamed: "I never said anything about marrying her. She knew what she was doing" (102). In time, according to Gaskell, she simply disappeared from his life. He assumes the masculine privilege of keeping his past closed, and even the shock of learning about the woman's death and Kiddie's birth gives him little insight into the consequences of his masculine point of view. He begs Frank to see that only her ideas separate them, and that her ideas bear little resemblance to the facts of natural differences between men and women, and to his impunity under the laws of his society. Under such laws, Gaskell can refuse to label his actions or beliefs wrong, and with his attitudes he can argue that Frank's love for him ought to blot out any other consideration. But Frank rejects the philosophy that "makes nature the excuse" for ruining a woman's life, and she ends their relationship. Gaskell exits from her apartment at the final curtain.

IV   *Barriers to Woman's Freedom*

The main theme of the play, the barriers to woman's freedom, is a characteristic Crothers theme which receives its most extensive development in this play. Aside from direct declarations or demonstrations of male power, Crothers also investigates the more indirect assertion of man's dominance through the rhetoric of chivalry. For example, the moment when Frank declares to Malcolm that her past is spotless, she becomes clothed for him "in a radiance," and he wishes to kneel and worship her. He regards his response as universal and inevitable: "That's the way all men feel towards good women and you can't change it" (99). Crothers supplies a less romantic conception of monogamy as a means to secure man's right to his property in Gaskell's later declaration that "a man wants the mother of his children to be the purest in the world" (99). Crothers does not emphasize the anthropological understanding of female chastity, as did many feminists, but she clearly was aware of the social necessity of woman's purity. Not content to know individually that Frank is a "good" woman, Gaskell proposes that she parade her virtue to the rest of the world, urging her to send Kiddie away to boarding school in order to leave no taint on herself.

Crothers also explores the indirect social tyranny of a man's world in the lives of two minor women characters. Lione Brune, the tempermental opera singer who foments suspicion against Frank, expresses a most cynical acceptance of male dominance which barely hides her repugnance of men. Once she recognizes that Frank is truly distressed by the rumors of Gaskell's resemblance to Kiddie, she counsels Frank to take a laissez-faire attitude toward men's prerogatives: "Men are pigs of course. They take all they can get and don't give any more than they have to. It's a man's world—that's the size of it. What's the use of knocking your head against things you can't change? I never believed before that you really meant all this helping woman business. What's the use? You can't change anything to save your neck" (94). When Frank suggests that women could change men's behavior by making them "equally disgraced for the same sin" that secured woman's downfall, Lione is quick to point out that masculine power has a chilling effect on woman's moral standards: "When it comes to morality, a woman never holds anything against a man. What good would it do if she did? She'd be alone" (94). She advises Frank simply to take Malcolm as he is, "and thank your lucky stars you have him" (95).

Lione puts up a front of independence, but her fear of being abandoned by men warps her values. Clara Oakes, Lione's roommate, is the picture of timidity and dependence, and as the third single woman artist in the house, her struggle in the man's world arouses pathos. She is thirty-seven, unattractive, and a mediocre artist. Although she has challenged the restrictions of her upper-class family and has broken with them to pursue her art, she is unable to reject the more subtle social values which tie her self-respect to the single success of marriage. After the failure of her exhibition to draw any rich commissions, Clara confesses to being so disheartened that she'd "marry anything that could pay the bills" (86). However, she recognizes that her problems arise as much from the general disadvantages of the female sex as from the presumably unattractive aspects of her person: "If I were a man—the most insignificant runt of a man—I could persuade some woman to marry me . . . and could have a home and children and hustle for my living and life would mean something" (86). Frank empathizes with Clara's unhappiness, but she rejects the philosophy that claims woman is nothing without a man, or that the most sexually exploited, "wicked" woman is better off than a man-less one. Instead, she encourages Clara to teach in one of her ghetto clubs, strengthened by her knowledge that life is "harder" for women generally than for men.

The play clearly reflects the sex hostilities and sex antagonisms which were prominent social phenomena, but it also avoids being a narrowly polemical interpretation of the society. Frank's feminism, for example, is flexible enough for her to recognize that not all women are ready for the freedom she demands. When Clara confesses that she is somewhat embarrassed to tell Frank that she wants to be protected, knowing that Frank believes in women helping themselves, Frank remarks that, indeed, Clara would have been far happier had she married as a young woman and that is not to her discredit. Similarly, Crothers

does not portray all aspects of female-male relations as degraded
or destructive. One of the play's deepest relationships exists
between Frank and Fritz Bahn, the gentle violinist who loves
her. Further, through Fritz's despair, we come to know how it
feels to be a man who has not measured up to the stringent code
of aggressive and successful masculinity in a male world. Finally,
the relations between Frank and Gaskell have some very
attractive aspects, especially at the beginning. As the two strong-
willed people spar for points and time, there is wit and humor in
their heated courtship.

Critical reactions to the play were usually mixed. There was an
almost universal appreciation for the "unhappy ending" with
Crothers separating her lovers rather than permitting love to
triumph above all;[9] at least one reviewer doubted the finality of
Frank's decision, concluding, "You cannot resist the feeling that
she will call him back again in a few days or weeks."[10] At the
same time, even generally favorable responses to the play
display a sense of unease with Frank's New-Woman character
and convictions. The *Toledo Blade,* for example, stressed the
typically feminine events in Frank's life, commenting on her
"maternal solicitude" to Kiddie, and her awakening to love, and
ultimately praised Mary Mannering, who played Frank, as such a
"womanly woman" that with her interpreting the role, "any
character could be made lovable." [11]

Some critics responded enthusiastically to Frank's high-
minded appeal for a single standard of morality, but most
rejected the proposal as ridiculously Utopian, emptyheadedly
feminine, or drably monotonous.[12] With the exception of Flexner,
very few critics, then or later, paid much attention to the larger
women's issues raised by the play, and some indirectly attacked
the theme of woman's independence and integrity by paying
undue attention to Clara's cry for marriage and protection as a
true indication of what women wanted, while ignoring Frank's
analysis of Clara's plight, or Lione's cynical assessment of male
power.[13]

Two points of criticism that require close attention are the
secrets and coincidences of the plot, and the implications
surrounding Frank's rejection of Gaskell. In regard to the former,
several critics have focused on what they charge to be
weaknesses of dramatic structure. Eaton, for example, praises
Crothers's "daring" choice of theme and her "daring handling of

it," but he argues that because of plot coincidences the play "misses the masculinity of structure and the inevitableness of episode necessary to make it dramatic literature."[14] Dickinson, in 1925, condemned the plot as mechanical and arbitrary, charging that it was not only "very old fashioned at this date" but even at the time it was first produced.[15] In regard to Frank's rejection of Gaskell, many critics took Crothers to task for simply reversing the discrimination against woman and applying an equally unjust punishment against man.

Although there is a long-standing critical disparagement of the well-made play, the conventions of this genre neither warp the logic of the action nor falsify or trivialize its content. Through the coincidences of Gaskell and Frank residing in the same boardinghouse, and through Frank's "discovery" of Gaskell's paternity via Kiddie's miniature, the theoretical opposition between the New Woman and her chauvinist fiancé becomes bitterly personal. Furthermore, such coincidences in a society whose economic and social institutions furthered illegitimacy, were a concern of numerous early modern plays, Ibsen's *Ghosts* and Shaw's *Mrs. Warren's Profession* being only two outstanding examples.

Finally, the implications of Frank's rejection of Gaskell are most important to clarify because the crucial factor is not that she rejects Gaskell on the basis of the past, but, rather, on the basis of what he stands for in the present. The dramatic structure helps us see this. When Frank discovers the truth about Malcolm at the end of Act Three, this discovery alone does not mark the end of their relationship. That turning point comes only in Act Four, when Gaskell maintains that his rights to dominance and his freedom from being accountable for his sexual activities are grounded in the "laws" of his world. When he urges Frank to put aside her ideas and capitulate to her emotions of love, he counsels a course which he himself refuses to take. Crothers saw Frank as a "modern woman" who thinks as well as feels, and who, in crises, "is ruled by reason."[16] Such a woman is inadmissible in Gaskell's code. The attack against Frank as a prude or a man-hater is as much a rejection of woman as a thinking creature as it is a rejection of her demand for a single moral standard.

A different sort of attack, briefly referred to in Quinn, came from Augustus Thomas's *As A Man Thinks* (1911), in which a society woman attempts to repay her husband's infidelity with an affair of her own and feels the lash of the double moral standard. Another woman character complains about "the privileges these men claim," and declares: "And that woman dramatist with her play was right. It is 'a man's world.' "[17] The hero of the play, a wise old Jewish doctor, counters the claims of woman's oppression with claims of woman's advantages: ". . . this is *a woman's world.* The great steamships dependable almost as the sun—a million factories in civilization—the countless looms and lathes of industry— the legions of labor that weave the riches of the world—all—all move by the mainspring of man's faith in woman—man's faith."[18] When woman betrays man's faith in her, she must be punished. According to Thomas, "The play tries to show that such punishment must persist so long as the family is the unit of our social structure,"[19] because only pure womanhood can guarantee man a legitimate family. Despite the objectivity of this argument, however, Thomas's antipathy to woman's progress emerged again in *Mere Man* (1912), in which he presents a case against woman's suffrage.

What makes the play a powerful experience even today, however, is not the content of Frank's ideas or philosophy, but the level of her consciousness of her struggle. Frank presumed she had cut men out off her life, and had thereby eliminated the possibility of feeling woman's pain in a man's world. Although at first she feels like a "traitor" to herself, she finally opens herself to loving Malcolm, and when she does so, she experiences the force of masculine power in an immediate and emotional way. Through the emotional complications surrounding her affair with Gaskell, Crothers portrays the conflicts of Frank's character: between her desire to submerge herself in the mind-evaporating power of the man's world, and her need to be true to the knowledge of her own consciousness. Ultimately Crothers denies her the comfortable niche she gave Bettina: to demand freedom and independence for other women from the comfortable security of her lover's arms. The power of romantic love falters in *A Man's World* because it is apparent to its heroine that relations between women and men are founded on injustices to women, a thesis that would likely meet with as little enthusiasm today as it did when Crothers first presented it.

V   *Other Early Work*

With *A Man's World,* Crothers broke some of the dictations of drama as diversion for the masses. Other projects from these years suggest that her theatrical perspective went beyond the boundaries of Broadway. In 1909, Crothers wrote *William Craddock* for the New Theatre in New York, an expensive prewar venture in noncommercial theater that failed after two seasons. The play was never produced, and there is no record of a typescript. Crothers also wrote two light-hearted dramatic vignettes which were published in 1909 in the *Smart Set,* Mencken and Nathan's urbane journal. "Katy Did" is a whimsical detective story which plays on the title both as a solution to the mystery and as the sound of the insect. "Mrs. Molly," a somewhat more interesting comedy sketch, argues that divorce is an inappropriate remedy for a husband's infidelity, since loneliness is worse for the wife than a philandering husband.

CHAPTER 3

Exploring the Impact of Feminism

I *Portrait of the Artist as a New Woman*

HE and She (1911) is Crothers's most complex and pessimistic exploration of feminism's impact on society, particularly on marriage and the family, and one of the best plays she wrote. Unlike *A Man's World* it is not an explicit or optimistic call to feminist action; on the contrary, what the play implies most strongly is the great distance still to be traveled before America would provide a hospitable climate for woman's freedom, and before American women would defeat the fears and guilts about freedom that lurked in their natures. Crothers focuses on the struggle of a woman to survive as an artist in a social milieu that erects barriers, both open and subtle, before talented women. Ann Herford, a wife and a mother, as well as a sculptor, faces mutually exclusive goals: to complete a sculpture that will publicly confirm her genius, or to take up a full-time role of guiding her teenaged daughter during a period of personal trauma. Numerous influences, both social and psychological, persuade Ann to abandon her career at its height and to protect her daughter. Once her decision is made in favor of her daughter, Ann writhes against the limitations on her progress. In structure and theme, Crothers's play is simple and unified. She distills the ordinary experiences of traditional woman's life as wife and as mother and plays them off against the struggles of her woman artist.

Because its production history is confusing, there are difficulties in assessing the contribution of *He and She* to the American stage and in evaluating its place in Crothers's career. *He and She* went through two years of tryouts on the road in attempting to gain a New York production. First seen as *He and She* in the fall of 1911, the play failed to convince commercial

50

managers of a profitable New York run. In 1912, Crothers renamed the play *The Herfords*, secured Viola Allen, a very popular actress, for the lead, and reorganized a road tryout, beginning in Boston. Crothers was hopeful that a new appreciation for serious drama would prove the managers wrong. "The public," she declared, was "away ahead of the managers," and wanted dramatists who would "give their best to the stage, the most important modern thinking of which they are capable. . . ."[1]

Crothers's hopefulness was raised, at least in part, because the Drama League, established in 1911, promised to raise the level of theater by educating American audiences to the finest of Continental and classical dramas, and by encouraging productions of American plays that could not succeed on the old commercial terms.[2] Indeed, the Boston chapter of the league invited Crothers to address them while *The Herfords* played in Boston, but it did not support the play, and Crothers's renewed effort failed once again to reach New York. Eight years later, once Crothers had established her reputation in the theater and the importance of succeeding on the road had declined, she revived *He and She* in New York, taking the lead herself. Subsequently, she revised the script for Quinn's *Representative American Plays*, and this is the source of the present discussion, since no earlier-dated version of the play can be confirmed.[3]

From Crothers's perspective, *He and She* represented "the progress of American drama" in a number of ways. Three of her women, for example, were in their thirties, and she exulted that "no more is it necessary to confine heroines to ingenues, stage age 17."[4] She also proposed that investigations of woman's life as the central material of drama were a great advance of the modern theater and no doubt envisioned her newest play as part of the avant-garde. In trying to understand why "most of the great modern plays are studies of woman," Crothers suggested that "women are in themselves more dramatic than men, more changing, and a more significant note of the hour in which they live because of their own evolution . . . the most important thing in modern life."[5] From an historical perspective, *He and She* shows the strong influence of Shaw and the drama of discussion. Most critics were not favorably disposed to this particular dramatic advance and Crothers faced the charge that her play was "all talk and no action," a charge frequently leveled by

American critics during the early part of the twentieth century.
    The setting of Crothers's three-act drama, a spacious old New York home, externalizes the ideal of Tom and Ann Herford, both sculptors, to forge an egalitarian marriage, free of the limitations of the stereotyped masterful male and the submissive female. Each has a studio in the basement of the home where Act One is set. Its ceiling is raised to double height to accommodate the couple's work, and to signal, perhaps, their less-confined domestic horizons. Other details of the couple's reorganization of their home and family life also reflect their modern ideals. Carpets, for example, have been replaced by tile floors for easier housekeeping; and the heavy, dark formality of Victorian homes has been replaced by light, flexible grace. Millicent, the Herfords' sixteen-year-old daughter, goes to boarding school, and when she is home for holidays she is obliged to respect Ann's need to work—something her father enforces. As the play progresses, however, and conflicts begin to restrict Ann's sphere, the setting enhances the play's theme. The action moves to the ground floor, where domestic activities prevail.
    The play is simply plotted around events which cause Ann to reevaluate her life as an artist. Two subplots, following the conflicts of two other women characters, enrich our understanding of Ann's conflict between her public aspirations and private duties and broaden the spectrum of women's dilemmas. At the end of Act One, Ann decides to enter a sculpture competition for which Tom is also vying, and although her decision surprises him, Tom eventually supports her move. The act ends with the couple shaking hands. When Ann wins the $100,000 prize, and Tom places second, his opposition to her mounts and reaches a climax near the end of Act Two. He accuses Ann of being dominated by ambition and selfishness, and he demands that she take up full-time domestic duties. Ann refuses him, while recognizing the danger to their marriage. The act ends, however, on Millicent's unexpected arrival from boarding school and her refusal to return. In Act Three, Ann finally learns that Millicent's hysteria and stubbornness are related to her romance with the boarding-school chauffeur. Millicent announces her decision to marry the man, but it is clear to Ann that Millicent has come home out of a need to be guided in her confusion. Ann blames herself for Millicent's trouble because, during a holiday period when Ann was working on the frieze, Millicent stayed at school and

obviously responded to the man out of loneliness. Once Ann becomes convinced that she alone can help Millicent, she decides to take her to Europe, and asks Tom to complete her sculpture.

II   *The Antifeminists' Arguments*

Throughout the play, Ann is the target of traditional prejudices against women, and newer arguments against the New Woman. Particularly, her success in a formerly all-male field raises the type of hostility and fear regarding woman's progress which May notes as a characteristic of prewar society in *The End of American Innocence*.[7] Allusions to contests, battles, and fights, which flavor the play with Social Darwinism, reinforce the notion that woman in the public sphere was seen primarily as man's competitor. One of the play's chief characters predicts: "The great battle of the future" will probably be between "the sexes for supremacy" (905), and given current indications of woman's success, the probable outcome of such a battle no doubt left many men, and women, uneasy.

The constant debate over woman's place and woman's nature forces an internal opposition within the Herford household, and Crothers threads both pro-and antifeminist arguments so deftly into the domestic routine that the woman question permeates her characters' lives and defines their personalities as well. By making opposing parties out of people who have strong personal ties, Crothers complicates the emotional component of a highly emotional issue. Further, the subjects of disagreement, no matter how theoretical at the beginning of a discussion, ultimately become very personal issues. Attitudes toward the women's movement, for example, clearly indicate how the individual reacts to changes in women's status. By far, the antifeminists are in the majority. Tom's assistant, Keith McKenzie; his sister, Daisy, who works as his secretary; and Ann's father, Dr. Remington; as well as Tom himself—each contributes ammunition to the attacks against the New Woman. Millicent, representing the younger generation, is so lacking in consciousness of woman's fight for freedom that she forecasts the diminishing strength of feminists. Only Ann, and Ruth Creel, Keith's fiancée, support feminist ideals and try to live by them.

Keith McKenzie, the arch chauvinist, is portrayed as an

example of human wreckage cast up by an overly competitive society. His self-respect has been very slowly healed by the stability of his job with Tom, but he is obviously the most fearful man in the play. His sour views on the progress and power of the New Woman reflect his fear of having to face an even larger area of competition and the loss of his comfort if growing numbers of women refuse to keep their places at home. He finds it difficult to believe that Tom actually likes Ann to be busy with her work, rather than with their home, because in his own case he deeply resents Ruth's success as a journalist and her stubborn refusal to give up her job to marry him. To Tom, Keith's notion that women are men's possessions is an out-of-date, "I want my girl by my own fireside to live for me alone" (898) attitude. But Keith sees his argument in a different context: "The world has got to have homes to live in, and who's going to make 'em if the women don't?" (898). Keith's views on woman's talent reflect his need to see women as inferior in at least some area. While he is willing to admit that Ann might have more imagination than Tom, he insists that her sculpture is far inferior: "When it comes to the real thing, she isn't *in* it with him. How could she be? She's a woman" (902). Keith's antifeminism is played so broadly as to be comic, and he cheerfully accepts the labels of antediluvian and selfish, claiming that he is like 95 percent of the men in America who are selfish enough to insist on protecting their women. The strength of his position becomes reinforced, however, during the quarrel between Tom and Ann, because Tom plays every note in Keith's antifeminist tune.

Daisy, Tom's bachelor sister, shares almost all of Keith's views. Her brusque, solid exterior disguises a most traditionally domestic woman, yearning to devote herself to a man, and thoroughly committed to the ideal that woman's happiness comes only through serving and nurturing him. For Daisy it is not so much a conviction that men are superior, but that they ought to be. She objects to Ann's work as an artist because she sees it as a threat to Tom's superiority, long before Ann is ever in direct competition with her husband. She also resents the fact that Millicent is in boarding school and charges Ann with neglect of her maternal duties. Daisy's anger stems mainly from her belief that she is being misrepresented by the image of the New Woman as independent, strong, and superior. Such a woman as Daisy may look the part, but she feels burdened by her independence, not liberated by it, and believes that most women share her views. What most women want, she argues, is "to be the nicest thing in the world to some man" (916), and to use their intelligence only "to make a home, to bring up children, and to keep a man's love" (916).

The third dissenting voice raised against the New Woman, that of Dr. Remington, has higher authority than Daisy's or Keith's, but Crothers treats this authority with a mixture of awe and dismay. Remington combines the dignity of his scientific status with a nostalgia for the more simple days before women began demanding change. He predicts domestic chaos if men and women continue to abandon sexual boundaries, and he sees woman's gains as man's losses. Ann's freedom to work, in particular, is purchased at the price of Tom's masculinity. He warns his son-in-law: "If you don't look out you'll be so mixed up you'll be upstairs keeping house and Ann will be downstairs keeping shop" (904). He charges that Ruth is so brilliant that she is at least "half a man" (906); and his ideal "normal" woman is Daisy because she has no "kinks" or "ambitions" outside of domestic goals and she despises the woman movement.

Most of Remington's arguments rest on a "law" of natural differences between men and women which determined their separate spheres—a scientific point of view against suffrage frequently voiced in current journals. Remington's theory of woman's psychology is an outstanding example of the irrefutable logic of the law of natural differences—provided, of course, that there is agreement about the validity of its basic premise. From Remington's perspective, woman's biology or "sex" has determined the fundamental and unchanging aspects of woman's personality, as "sensitive," "involved," and "complex" (905). Modern society has allowed woman to exercise masculine personality traits by permitting her to work in the world, but work is nevertheless the man's sphere. Remington foresees an inevitable clash when "woman's nature becomes entangled in the responsibilities of a man's work" because "the two things [will] fight for first place in her—she's got a hell of a mess on hand" (905).

III *The Motherhood Question*

The idealization of motherhood, and its dominant place in woman's identity, are, finally, the most powerful arguments in the play. These arguments were not only unassailable weapons in the antifeminist arsenal but were used by feminists as well, who argued that woman's unique abilities as child-bearer and homemaker were needed in the public sphere as well as in the private. To the New Woman, however, the practical problems surrounding the place of motherhood in woman's identity were paramount, in light of her eagerness to make her mark in the world, and the play deals with the practical side of the dilemma less crisply and less critically than it does with other issues centering on modern woman's changing status.

Remington idealizes the maternal figure sitting by the fireside with children on her lap and prescribes motherhood as "the only thing in the game that's worth a cent" for women (922). Child-bearing is "as near divinity" as humans ever come, and women, particularly his daughter, who are tempted away from this woman's happiness by "the new restlessness and strife" of the world—the era's catchphrase for feminism—are being blinded to "the old things—the real things" (924). On the other hand, Ruth announces that "being a mother is the most gigantic and thankless thing in the world" (911), and she wants none of it. In comparison to the excitement and challenge of her work, caring for a baby full-time would bore her. From Remington's point of view, Ruth would be a prime example of his belief that the restlessness and ambition of modern woman have taken her on a dangerously deviant course.

IV   *The Feminists Fight Back*

In order to refute the arguments and pressures against the New Woman, Ann and Ruth present their side of the case. Both women deny the basic premises that woman's nature is unchanging and that her domestic role is her only reason for existing. By redefining woman's nature away from the "emotional" and "domestic animal" of earlier generations, they hope to gain acknowledgment for the obvious achievements of the newer generation of women. Both women agree on the unquestioned benefits to woman of economic independence, and while Ann has reorganized her family and home life to complement her work, Ruth has reduced so severely the importance of domesticity in her life that Keith cannot imagine how their future home can ever be comfortable. In comparing the women's critical perceptiveness of the subtle social barriers to woman's progress, Ruth's awareness exceeds Ann's on many questions. She is convinced, for example, that the men around her have limited Ann's talent by treating her as a clever lady sculptress, when, in fact, Ann is a woman of genius who ought to "resist everything" that threatens her genius (908). She is aghast when Ann creates secret models for Tom, to replace the designs he plans to enter in the contest. Ann is convinced that Tom's work is weak, yet she never questions whether her talents ought to be in the service of his fame, until Tom rejects her criticism, and her models, with patronizing compliments.

On the question of the status of motherhood, in woman's life, both women seem bound by their era's social reality, just beginning to be redefined in contemporary society, that child care is the sole responsibility of woman. They make no attempt to redefine the role of mother, nor to relate the subject to questions of woman's sphere or nature. Ruth ultimately breaks her engagement to Keith and disappears from the play in the crucial last act, so her preference for childlessness disappears as an alternative life-style in the play. Ann, however, as wife and mother, must confront the demands of both roles as they threaten to limit her life as an artist, and, indeed, the play builds to two high points around these conflicts. The first major confrontation, with Tom, results in Ann's thorough rejection of the doctrine that man is the ruler of the home, and that woman must subordinate herself to his demands. Once Ann wins the prize, Tom is jealous and fearful but hides these emotions behind a screen of righteous demands. Tom insists, for example, that in order for Ann to prove she loves him and Millicent more than her work, she must give up her commission. Ann tells him that her love has been based on his freedom from oppressive masculine dominance. "I want to believe you're what I thought you were," she tells him. "Don't make me think you're just like every other man" (921). When Tom's rightful authority as husband does not work, he finally threatens Ann that unless she comes back "to the things a woman's always had to do and always will, we can't go on ... you're a woman and I'm a man. You're not free in the same way..." (921).

Ann refuses to yield to Tom's threats or to his arguments, a decision the play later supports when Tom recognizes the selfishness of his position and asks Ann to forgive him. By this means Crothers dismisses neither Tom's anger nor the intensity of his fear, but she does acknowledge that woman's progress implies monumental social and individual changes. Tom feels as if "something sort of gave way under my feet" when he learned that Ann had won (923). But Crothers's sympathy for Tom does not extend to his specious arguments. At the core of his assertion of contrasting freedom for the sexes lies the care and feeding of his ego and the proprietary nature of his claims on Ann. She strips away the respectability of his charges of Ann's selfishness and shows that Tom, instead, is the selfish party.

Ann's second crucial reevaluation of her life as an artist comes when she must decide on the importance of Millicent's life in her own life. Crothers presents Ann's final dilemma as a central one for the New Woman: determining the point at which her rightful regard for self becomes the abnormal selfishness with which her critics charged her. At the critical point there can be little wonder that Ann comes to Millicent's aid: Tom has no patience with his daughter, and Ann sees she needs help. What is surprising is Ann's rationale for helping Millicent; she accepts almost wholly the charges of selfishness which had been laid against her and which she had resisted from the beginning of the play. Ann decides to drop the commission when she hears Millicent's love story and connects the time she has devoted to her art to Millicent's trouble. She convinces Millicent that she is so overworked that only an extended European voyage and her daughter's company can overcome her exhaustion. Although Millicent is reluctant to delay her marriage, she agrees to accompany her mother, since the need is so clear, and tells Ann that she could never be so "selfish" as to deny her mother's wish. Her speech strikes the key note of selfishness, a note which reverberates in Ann's explanation to Tom that she is shifting her priorities now because she realizes that she "was pushing Millicent off" (928). In coming to that recognition, Ann uses the phrases of those who equate woman's identity with motherhood: devoting full time to Millicent is her job, because Millicent is "what I've given to life. If I fail her now—my whole life's a failure" (928).

V   Barriers to Woman's Progress

Ann's struggle to work as an artist clearly dominates the play, both in terms of theme and structure, and in her characterization as well. Built up from the play's beginning, Ann's portrait as an artist makes a memorable impression that lasts throughout later scenes when she weighs her personal life against her public one. Crothers immediately impresses us with Ann's work from her first entrance on stage. She is wearing "a long linen working smock—a soft rich red in color. Her sleeves are rolled up ... she is at work" (908). On Ann's second entrance, she emerges from her workroom carrying a newly finished nude of a woman. She graciously declines Tom and Keith's offer to help her carry the heavy sculpture; she teases her father out of his displeasure with a vocation that leads Ann to fashioning naked ladies rather than caring for her daughter; and she gives an instant hearing to Millicent's demand that Ann organize a holiday dinner for several of her boarding-school friends. Through the creation of this milieu, and the selection of the casual and petty threads of day-to-day living, Crothers sensitively portrays the many small but real barriers to women as artists.

Crothers's use of the stage underscores the antagonisms inherent in Ann's decision to take her art as seriously as Tom takes his. Crothers executes the scene at the close of Act One by emphasizing the social estrangement of Ann's decision to enter the contest. At the moment of her decision, Ann stands stage right, facing her husband, her father, and Keith, who form an incredulous chorus (910). The men demand that Ann justify her surprising move, and her reasons come in disconnected revelations, until Ann recognizes with some surprise the deep source of her own needs: "I want it with my whole soul. ... It means more to me than I can possibly—why shouldn't I? I want to" (910). Only Tom ultimately breaks ranks with the men to wish Ann good luck.

In the play's final scene, there is something of a reversed repetition of the end of Act One. Instead of being overwhelmed by joy and excitement, Ann struggles with anger and resentment while ironically threaded through are Tom's apologies for his jealousy, and his insistence that Ann must have the public glory of her triumph: "My God, you've not only beaten me—you've won over the biggest men in the field—with your own brain and your own hands in a fair, fine, hard fight" (928). He's convinced now that Ann's decision to aid Millicent will backfire because she will be overwhelmed by regrets and the "artist in you will *yell* to be let out" (928), but he agrees to "do whatever she wants," and so will complete the sculpture.

Ann, of course, knows very well the depth of her need to

achieve as an artist. She has felt the pride of accomplishment when people looked at the "strong" men and women of her sculpture and remarked, "A woman did that," a pride she feels for herself and for "*all* women" (928). She also recognizes that her own anger will be directed to a variety of targets: "I'll hate you because you're doing it—and I'll hate myself because I gave it up—and I'll almost—hate—her" (928).

The angry mood surrounding Ann's dilemma is heightened in the final gestures and lighting of the play. Once Ann confirms the finality of her decision, she and Tom embrace in the first harmonious gesture between husband and wife since their Act-One handshake. Ann moves out of the embrace, and her final words, "Put out the light," echo Othello's mournful intonation as he has decided to kill Desdemona. Ann's final statement is the weary, "I hope she's asleep," and as the room darkens about them, husband and wife move to the small lighted area of the hall, further backstage, and the figure of Ann recedes into domesticity.

The larger social barriers to woman's progress can be seen in the contrasting fates of Crothers's New Women. Ann's "voluntary" decision to withdraw from the competition effectively removes her from the male arena. As for Ruth, the consequence of her cleverness is that she is no longer eligible for romance or for marriage. Since she cannot compromise on her freedom, she breaks her engagement and exits from the marriage market, clearing the way for traditional woman, Daisy, to have her chance. As Daisy tells Keith, he has no right to ask Ruth to give up her work. After all, Ruth is "more clever in her way than you are in yours. She'll go further, and if you can make her stop, she'll hate you some day because she'll think you've kept her back" (916).

From the play's perspective, then, woman's chances for synthesizing a new role from her theoretical freedom are far more limited than the rhetoric of freedom might suggest. In Crothers's play no man loses his identity as a person when he becomes a husband or a father, nor does he have to choose between private or public life.[8] In Crothers's depiction, however, the best, most talented representatives of modern womankind are either melted down in the crucible of marriage or maternity, or else they are denied both experiences. The society in which these dramas are acted out is not the crass man's world of her earlier play, but potentially more damaging and more limiting; sex antagonism is only the tip of the social iceberg, and Crothers's play just begins to plumb the depths of guilt and fear which have fomented the unhappiness in the play.

VI   *The Critics Take Sides*

Despite the play's ambiguities and complexities, the earliest criticism of the play reflected the most prominent social concern: the debate between career and home. Of the few reviews available from the earliest production of *He and She*, all agree that Crothers's play was an argument for woman remaining in her domestic sphere, although critics split between favoring and opposing this position. The *Boston Transcript*, while noting the purpose of the play was "to enforce on women the importance of their work as mothers and homemakers," argued that although the play shows "that woman's neglect of the home may cause havoc," it is simply a "single case," and no proof that "the movement of women into what have been men's occupations must stop."[9] In contrast the critic of the *Atlanta Constitution* described Ann's problem as her being "so devoted to her art that she fails to see its incongruousness in her life." Thus it applauded the "rude jolt" the play delivered to the proponents of "woman and her enlarging sphere," by showing that Ann finally achieves "what is noblest in her . . . mother love and her woman's power of sacrifice."[10]

Even the acting of the play was affected by polarized social views. The *Boston Transcript*, for example, claimed that Jessie Izette's performance of Ruth Creel turned Ruth into an "unsympathetic burlesque," even though the character is "clearly and truthfully drawn and her position honestly stated."[11] Similarly, we might infer that Viola Allen's portrayal of Ann reflected her own ambivalence about the role of modern woman. She viewed the play as being "about the question whether the profession of a married woman is not the greatest in the world," and asserted that "the best thing a woman can be is a mother."[12] Further, the broadening of woman's horizons, "far from reducing her effectiveness as a mother, actually made her a better mother." Nevertheless, Allen argued against marriage as the one aim in woman's life; after all, "plenty of spinsters are not only happy but valuable to the world because of the work or talent that makes their unmarried existence anything but a drear waste." Perhaps Miss Allen recalled that the author of her starring vehicle was not, indeed, a married woman.

Commentary on the New York revival in 1920 is more plentiful and suggests that a period of eight years broadened critical opinions about the play's theme. Heywood Broun accepted the play as a lesson against woman in public life but found the lesson unconvincing and tiresome. He humorously announced his intention "to write a pro-feminist play in which the young girl of the house marries a street cleaner because her mother is so busy baking apple pies that she has no time to take proper care of her daughter."[13] Burns Mantle called the play's problem "insoluble ... until generations of men and women yet unborn have struggled with it," and even then he had doubts about finding a solution.[14] Alexander Woollcott refuted the play as an argument for woman's domestic preferences because Ann "is already a wife and a mother." He suggested, instead, the social dimensions of Ann's conflict when he classified the play as a tragedy on the grounds that "something fine and strong dies in the last act. It is the hope, the ambition and all the future work of a genius— deliberately slain, in order that the 'she' of 'He and She' may be able to play more attentively and more wholeheartedly what she is driven to regard as her more important role—that of wife and mother."[15]

Contemporary sources have clouded the play's theme. Garff Wilson's summary in *Three Hundred Years of American Drama and Theater* records that Ann is "shocked and incredulous to discover that Tom will not subordinate himself to helping her, as she would have done had Tom won."[16] Jordan Miller's reference to the play as "a rival to Mitchell's *The New York Idea* as an early high comedy"[17] suggests an interesting ideological clash between the two plays, but overlooks the serious tone and sacrificial ending of Crothers's drama. Yvonne Shafer is more accurate about the play's tone, calling it a "pessimistic appraisal" of Ann's difficulties in maintaining a career and a marriage,"[18] but by calling Millicent's problem "contrived" and the ending "weak" she ignores the burden of the play, which is the irrefutable call to women to care for children and not for their husbands' egos.

Crothers's own comments on her drama shed some interesting light on the career-versus-home debate, although the comments are incomplete. Shortly after the production of *A Man's World,* Crothers talked of an idea for her next play, about "a girl who goes out into the world to make her career. She goes jeering at the idea of home and husband. Her jeers are heard by a little home woman, and they make her dissatisfied with her lot. After a while, the woman comes back. She finds the little woman unhappy and tells her she has the better part."[19] No doubt, the kernel of Ruth's character and the conflict between Ruth and Daisy are suggested by this brief résumé. What Crothers finally produced in Ann's struggle, however, was something different.

In a contemporaneous news item, Crothers described the subject of her play as "the restlessness of women" in modern society, but she diverged from most reviewers' conclusions by stating that her play does not argue that "talent should always sacrifice itself to domesticity." Nevertheless, she brings her character "to a crisis where she must choose between her artistic ambition and her daughter's happiness. . . ."[20] Although the article lacks any conclusions about the relative merits of the "home woman" and the "new woman," Crothers finally does suggest that women who stay at home could be living more "worthwhile" lives rather than "being merely the . . . consumers they now are."

There is also, of course, the unsolved question of what changes *He and She* went through from the time of its first production to the shape of the present text and of whether the changes signal Crothers's more successful realization of her dramatic intention. One possibility is that Crothers became more aware of the problems she had uncovered regarding Tom's attitude toward Ann's talent. We can compare a report of the 1912 production with the present text of the scene when Ann expresses doubts about the quality of Tom's entry to the sculpture competition and then shows him her models. In the later version, Tom is essentially critical of the feminine grace of Ann's designs, and he rejects her offer to give them to him as a substitute entry. In the earlier version, we are told that Ann "herself has had an idea for the prize frieze and has made the preliminary drawings. She spreads her drawings before him and he is astonished. 'It is beautiful!' he exclaims: 'I'm not sure it is not great!' He urges her to try for the prize and the curtain falls."[21]

The play obviously has yielded interpretations that support either pro-or antifeminist sentiments and might still do so today.[22] Perhaps the play's special value lies in its rendering of women's lives, each having its own integrity, drawing on the strength of each woman's needs and dreams; the women are special not so much because they are pulled by the forces of their day, but because each life is lived in a conviction of its necessity. The forces of the day are sufficiently embedded in the character's personality to be convincing, whether it is a force for change or a force for the status quo. The play lacks the revolutionary fervor of *A Man's World;* indeed, Crothers seems to have been careful not to make villains out of people whose views were exposed as dangerous or destructive. But what the play lacks in focused ardor it makes up for in the possibilities it raises that women's freedom will come only at the high price of social isolation, and that woman's life in the modern world is shaped more by the limits on her freedom than by any newly won independence.

The inescapable impact of the play is the strength of resistance to changes in women's roles. Crothers's feminists are isolated and subjected to such casual and good-natured abuse that we are forced to acknowledge the respectability of the antifeminist stance, even to Dr. Remington's offhand use of the misogynist rhyme: "A woman, a dog, and a walnut tree; the more you beat 'em, the better they be" (923).

VII   *Other Restless Women*

In comparison with some of the contemporaneous stage presentations of woman's restlessness, Crothers contributed an in-depth rendering of the human, rather than the theatrical, price of woman's struggle for freedom. Of the three restless women in Clyde Fitch's successful *The City* (1910), one is murdered by her dope-crazed lover; a second rejects her belief in her own happiness and assumes responsibility for reuniting with her philandering husband; and the third comes to regret all aspects of her modern life and freedom. A much-praised later rendering of modern woman's accomplishments was James Forbes's *The Famous Mrs. Fair* (1919), with which Crothers's revival of *He and She* was frequently compared. It presents a striking group portrait of active and vigorous women who triumphed in military work during World War I, but portrays Nancy Fair's postwar involvement in public life as a sign that she is displaying her ego and her selfishness, and not that she is accomplishing any good.

Crothers's drama remains a superior exposition of the clash between woman's freedom and the psychological and social limitations to that freedom. It takes its place, along with *A Man's World*, as one of the best pieces in the Crothers canon, both for its forceful characterizations and for its clear portrayal of the barriers to women as artists. In its test of woman's freedom to succeed within the context of home and family, it proves home and family incompatible with total freedom and tells women to make their choice in the clear light of knowing the options before them.

VIII   Reforming Prostitutes and Good Women

In *Ourselves* (1913), Crothers pursued her conviction that American audiences would support a dramatist's "most modern thinking," and dealt with the very current topic of America's great social evil—prostitution. The four-act play survived only twenty-nine performances in its New York production, but the attention it attracted as a "sociological drama" and a "modern vice play" suggests the continuing American interest in "plays with a punch,"[23] and documents the increasing frankness with which social problems were being portrayed on stage.[24] Her opening act, portraying an outcast class of women in a New York reform home, is an excellent example of American naturalism, authentic not only in external details but in underlying emotions.

In order to experience firsthand some part of the prostitute's reality, Crothers visited police courts and the Bedford State Reformatory.[25] The play also testifies that Crothers was widely read on her subject, since the explanations of the social roots of prostitution include poverty, drugs, poor education, and the naiveté of immigrant women, the lack of healthy entertainments for working girls in large cities, as well as the actual practices of white slavery, all of which were part of the progressive social analysis of her day. Crothers's treatment of the prostitutes' social origins is brief, although explicit, and she concentrates on the moral climate in which prostitution flourishes. In addition, she searches the personality of her young, rootless courtesan, Molly, a product of the urban streets, for clues about her stubborn dependence on and loyalty to the man who put her on the streets. Crothers sets Molly's values in relief against the competing values of Beatrice Barrington, a wealthy woman interested in the reform movement. The two women have a clear impact on each other's lives by the end of the play.

The action of the play focuses on Beatrice's attempts to reform Molly by introducing her to a decent, tranquil, but to Molly, utterly boring, existence as a companion-secretary living in the Barrington home. The only condition of Molly's employment is that she keep away from her man, Leever, for a month, during which time she attempts to improve herself through voice lessons, penmanship exercises, and other worthwhile tasks. Despite her boredom, Molly is impressed with the benefits of an orderly life, and by the time she sees Leever again she is so caught up in visions of decency—including their marriage, his steady work, and a flat with a kitchen where she can put into practice her newly learned homemaking skills—that the man doubts her sincerity. He takes her month's wages and beats her. This encounter cures Molly of her idealized romance with her pimp, but her sexual energy and her need to belong to a man make her easy prey to the next man who charms her—Beatrice's married brother. Bob Barrington, an artist as well as a ladies' man, has all the advantages of wealth, position, and a promising career that Leever lacked, yet his cruelty to Molly, while not physical, is more punishing than the tough guy's, for he uses and discards Molly with absolutely no acknowledgment that she is a human being.

The action builds to the discovery of Molly's affair with Bob. Beatrice is crushed that Molly has upset her theory of reform and trampled on her generosity and kindness. In a highly emotional scene at the end of Act Three, she throws the sobbing Molly away from her, and denies her any sympathy or understanding. Bob's wife takes the news of his affair as an opportunity to protest against the dual moral standard—a code to which she had previously subscribed as in keeping with her modern moral sophistication. She rejects Bob's masculinist justification for his affairs, and rejects Bob as well. Beatrice is also taken aback by Bob's enunciation of his code and she recognizes her own abuse of Molly, falling into the trap that heaps blame on the woman while ignoring the man. By the play's end, though Molly prepares to leave the Barrington household, there is mutual affection expressed by the two women, and mutual agreement that Molly can achieve her desired decency only by working out her own destiny.

Through the course of the play, Crothers attempts to bridge the moral and economic gap between "good" women and their "fallen" sisters by showing that "good" women, far from having any right to dismiss the poor woman of easy virtue, have a moral responsibility for her plight: it is their well-bred indifference or ignorance which gives the men in their lives a free field for sexually exploiting poor women. As she weighs the merits of a number of solutions applied to the problems of regenerating prostitutes, Crothers exposes the uselessness of reforming prostitutes when the men who patronize them, the more appropriate targets of reform, receive no attention.

This perspective is expressed in a number of ways, most succinctly, perhaps, by Molly, who claims: "I ain't got much education to see there's something *wrong*. The men are runnin' after us and we get pinched" (II, 19). The matron of the reform home sets this injustice in the larger context of the problems of reform. She notes that although homes such as hers can save "a few girls," all the time and money spent on reform is "like dipping the water out of the ocean with a spoon. . . . What's the use of shutting up a few hundred girls a year," she asks, "while the men are running around loose looking for more? Once we take to locking up man—we'll get somewhere, not before" (I, 17).

The alternative to jailing men, as the play sees it, is to abolish the respectability of the masculine code that justifies their sexual behavior on the grounds that the male animal has an uncontrollable sexual appetite while the woman is chaste precisely because she has no sexual urges. Bob Barrington speaks for the man's standpoint when he tells his angry and pregnant wife that his affairs are irrelevant to their relationship and mean nothing "personal" to him. Irene is a "cold-blooded saint" (IV, 8) who could not understand his feelings because "your pulses beat evenly and slowly. You don't know what a man resists. . . . You're good because you don't want to be anything else—you couldn't if you tried" (IV, 8). But Irene denies the theory of woman's natural chastity and insists that she, too, has a sexual drive, but she has committed herself to her husband, and to monogamy, and therefore controls her drives. Now that she wants to be assured of Bob's loyalty and love, she refuses to echo the man's standpoint, claiming, "I've stifled and choked and hidden my fears about you. I've cackled the same stuff about a man's nature that most women do, but I know now they're all lies" (IV, 9). Even Collin, Beatrice's fiancé, who has been opposed to her reform work, ultimately has his eyes opened. He tries to argue with Bob that "the same old men's excuses" are "crooked. ... We go on bluffing about the rights of nature. Nature be damned. ... It's up to us to control it. Nothing else gets ahead of us. ... The only thing on earth we give up to and say we can't help is the brute in us ..." (IV, 5). The play, then, raises the question of human sexuality, and its relationship to social problems. As the matron of the reform home puts it, everything in a poor girl's background predisposes her to having more problems than a rich girl, "but *the* reason, back of it all, is that the sex attraction is the strongest thing in the world, and if people aren't taught what to do with it, they'll go *wrong*" (I, 13).

Thus, what Crothers's play demonstrates is that the poor girl's healthy sexual appetite is distorted by cheap thrills and lures; while there may be, indeed, cases of white slavery, the more usual route to destruction is that taken by a lonely and poor woman exploited by a man; as her dependence on him grows, going on the streets for him seems a lesser price than being abandoned. Molly's history bears out the characteristics of such a woman. Illegitimate and poor, she left home when a boarder in her mother's home was promised Molly's sexual favors as part of his board. In view of her history, the play lacks some credibility by leaping from Molly's background to Beatrice's insistence that good women are really responsible for prostitution, but its theme of woman's freedom still rings strongly. Crothers is concerned to free poor women from the confines of social prisons, and to free all women from the domination of the "man's standpoint," which consigns lower-class women like Molly to a category of "irrelevant" sexual objects and consigns "good" women to hypocritical pretense and silent suffering.

Crothers's play was revolutionary neither in theme nor in subject; indeed, the American stage had been rather flooded with what the critics referred to as "sex plays," capitalizing on the sensational aspects of current accounts of white slavery. But as a serious effort to deal with the subject, Crothers's play might have had a longer stage career, or at least been available in print, had she received some attention from the Drama League. As a critic on the *New York City Tribune* put it, "Here was a piece written, it would be supposed, directly at the superior and discerning individuals who compose the Drama League ... a play ... that brings to Broadway ideas and ideals seldom encountered there. The spectator may not share these ideals, he may object that the play is special pleading, but he cannot escape the fact that here is a work of unusual distinction; red hot with conviction and taken right out of the air that thinking and responsible Americans breathe ... *Ourselves* needed help, precisely the sort of help the Drama League is supposed to give, and which it in this case refused."[26]

In terms of critical reception, appreciation ran higher for Grace Elliston, who played Molly, than for the play as a whole, though most critics declared the act in the reform home effective and original, and most critics applauded the play's straightforward expression of the problem. There was the objection, however, that the play had nothing to teach the young because it didn't "warn" them against anything and even suggested that abstract moral lessons were useless.[27] A further objection was that, as one critic put it, "the voting half of the species had all the worst of it" in the debate.[28] Another critic preferred Crothers's argument for a single moral standard in *A Man's World* because in that play she wrote "frankly from the woman's point of view," which she did well, whereas in the Act Four quarrel between Irene and Bob, only Irene states her convictions convincingly, while Crothers "puts in only half the defense that any clear-thinking man could muster to such an occasion."[29]

From a contemporary point of view, the play's interest may be limited. The problem of the play—reforming prostitutes—holds less interest for a modern audience than it had for Crothers's peers. Further, the moral and didactic rendering of the problem makes it even less palatable. Miss Carew informs Beatrice about prostitution in a stilted, textbook rhetoric. She even remarks at one point: "Records show that almost every first fall comes because a girl's been fooled and deceived" (I, 13). Molly's final line, "I'd like to tell every girl on earth what I know now" (IV, 11), is more effective for getting the curtain to come down on a strong line than in clarifying her character. Further, weak characterization mars the play, particularly Beatrice's colorless fiancé, Collin, whose presence makes no impact either on Beatrice's life or on the audience, and who seems to be used to illustrate the possibilities of a man holding reformist sentiments.

Molly's characterization also is flawed. Until Act Two, Molly's personality is the drama's strongest feature, and Crothers plays off to good advantage the contrast between her lively coarseness, her penchant for flashy fashions, and her unruly hair, and Beatrice's cool dignity and earnestness. One of the play's best moments shows Molly addressing envelopes to Beatrice's friends, inviting them to attend a lecture on the "Moral Responsibility of the Individual Towards Society," and wistfully thinking about having fun. Although Crothers takes her reform seriously, she is able to poke fun at some of the more somber aspects of her reformer, and she does this mainly through Molly.

By Act Three, however, once Molly's affair with Bob Barrington has been under way for some weeks, she is sapped of her defiance and her humor. Giving herself totally to Bob, in the mistaken belief that he loves her, is quite credible, given Molly's deep need to have someone of her own; but what lacks credibility is that Molly could be so cowed by this affair, that she allows herself literally to be pushed to the side while Bob and Irene debate the place of a mistress in a man's life in their Act Four quarrel. What adds to the diffuseness of Molly's character in the last two acts is that Crothers really shifts the focus from Molly's regeneration to Irene's conversion from the man's standpoint. Crothers is thus able to make a broader point about the power of the masculinist code, but she loses the clarity that would have come with a consistent focus on Molly.

The play is unique in the Crothers canon, being her only effort to employ what she called a "photographic" style and a muckraking perspective.[30] Equally rare, but in keeping with her attempt to document the realities of the problem, there are several scenes of physical violence in the play, including a brawl between two inmates of the women's reform home in Act One. The play is also uncharacteristically heavy, weighted by a serious tone and a didactic intent, totally unrelieved by any of Crothers's usual romantic tangles.

Despite its weaknesses, however, the play remains laced with sharp perceptions about the social nature of human beings.

Crothers recognizes not only Molly's lack of education but Beatrice's lack of worldly knowledge. The sordid details of Molly's past, for example, come pouring out of her, not to Beatrice, but to the Barrington housekeeper, a working-class woman with whom Molly can identify. Molly's alienation from Beatrice also is a function of her feeling more like an "experiment" and less like a person to her benefactress. Altogether, the character of Molly makes *Ourselves* a most unusual Crothers play, and represents both the height and the finale of her career as a social-problem playwright.

IX *Poking Fun at Advanced Feminism*

Theater magazine had labeled *Ourselves* "among the plays of the feminist movement,"[31] but in the play that followed, *Young Wisdom* (1914), Crothers was both condemned and applauded for her satire of feminism. The play is as light, swiftly paced, and romantically complicated as *Ourselves* is somber and naturalistic. It met with generally greater critical favor than its predecessor, but it did not satisfy New York audiences and closed after fifty-six performances. The general subject of Crothers's play, emancipated womanhood, permits her to range over a number of current social critiques of monogamy, the double standard, the social implications of marriage, motherhood, and human sexuality, advanced subjects that foreshadowed the postwar revolution in manners and morals. Indeed, Crothers accounted for the play's failure on the grounds that it demanded more awareness of advanced thinking than her typical New York audience had: "Not enough people knew the facts, so the situation of the trial marriage seemed preposterous."[32] At the same time, as her title implies, she foreshadows the generational split which was to be a prominent postwar concern.

The three-act comedy, set among a privileged and professional urban family, combines aspects of the comedy of manners, with the traditional romantic comedy of intrigues and complication. The plot focuses on two sisters, Victoria and Gail Claffenden, played by the sister acting team of Edith and Mabel Taliaferro, and follows Victoria's successful, but temporary, conversion of her younger sister to feminism. Victoria's radical idealism has been nurtured in a college environment, whereas

Gail's life has been bound by her family environment, of which
the prominent features are an authoritarian judge for a father,
and a kindly, self-effacing woman for a mother. Thus, Gail's
forthcoming and highly ceremonious marriage to her rich beau,
Peter, is a product of her parents', particularly her father's,
prescription of what is socially acceptable for women.

Because Gail is not really in love with Peter and has been
going along with the marriage plans out of inertia, she is ripe for
Victoria's critique of marriage; eventually, the two women
pressure their conservative, reluctant beaux into experimenting
with a trial marriage in an isolated cabin. This backfires when
the Bohemian artist who occupies the cabin condemns their
"revolutionary experiment." He has fallen in love with the
younger sister, and almost destroys Peter for luring the innocent
into a sex trap. He takes the young people back to civilization
where the comic spirit prevails. The girls acknowledge that they
are disenchanted with the practical results of their advanced
theories. The lovers end up in appropriately loving pairs: the
rejected lover, Peter, drives the two couples to be married,
legally, and Mrs. Claffenden accompanies the joyful group,
giving the stamp of her social approval. No one remains an
outsider, except for the churlish Judge Claffenden.

Through this plot, Crothers satirizes the attitudes and beliefs
of the avant-garde by contrasting the intensity of their
pronouncements with the slightness of the Claffenden sisters.
Their "conversion" to feminism is obviously tenuous, based on an
intellectual fashion, and easily reversed.

Although only a small proportion of the play's time is devoted
to an examination of controversial issues, nevertheless Crothers's
portrayal of Victoria and her beliefs gives some insights into the
target of Crothers's satire. Victoria is intelligent, educated,
attractive, and earnest. She has vowed not to marry her beau,
Christopher, until five years after her graduation, a conviction
held by all the members of her college female society. She
believes in the necessity for women to establish a life independent of men, and to reject the false myths of romance. Victoria
believes in basing marriage on a sound rational footing by means
of trial marriage, and for a good part of the first act, she regales
her unenlightened younger sister by reading choice selections
from the writings of the most advanced social and sexual

philosophers of her day. Gail learns that the materialist displays
of current wedding celebrations clearly expose the culture's
"market-place" mentality. She learns that the call of her senses
takes precedence over her obligation to follow traditional moral
strictures on her behavior. And, ultimately, she is converted to
the notion that "trial" marriage is the only ethical action to take
in modern society.

Victoria has been particularly impressed with the logic of the
argument that "law" and "fear" keep husbands bound to wives, a
condition which degrades women and contaminates relations
between the sexes. Only when man freely stays with woman
because he loves and respects her can relations between the
sexes be "pure" and "noble." Victoria recognizes that her
"shocking" and "radical" program will attract only very strong
women, since most women are still in thrall to outworn social
norms. But Victoria's faith in her sex rests on woman's
fearlessness and greater ability to evolve: "The future of the
world depends on women. They are so much less afraid of the
new—the daring things—than man. Men don't evolute at all, you
know. They're now just about the way they have always been.
And women have grown and grown and grown out of one stage
into another till they've reached the place where they must lead
men" (I, 7).

The opposition to Victoria's arguments appears both in the
action of the play, as the trial marriage scheme sours, and in the
arguments of Mrs. Claffenden. The mother appears to be the
prototype of the abused, oppressed housewife, cowed by her
overbearing husband. Despite this appearance, however, by Act
Three Mrs. Claffenden has, somewhat incredibly, gained a new
strength and status as the speaker of traditional values. Once her
daughters return home from their escapade, their mother
challenges their thinking and rejects the notion that the younger
generation has achieved any advances. Mrs. Claffenden insists
that nothing new has been discovered about women, despite
Victoria's conviction that her books contain revolutionary
insights. Mrs. Claffenden suggests that radical feminism is simply
a substitute for woman's normal life and wonders: "If one of
these free women had married a good commonplace man and
borne three children and stuck to him and watched her children
grow up with a mother's love to help them—had seen her

husband come into a position of honor and with him had come to represent the peace and dignity and happiness of family life. . . . I wonder if she couldn't have something to say on the one side about living for others as well as for one's self and I wonder, after all, which in the end brings the deeper happiness" (III, 12).

Although the play seems to use the debate over advanced philosophies only as a take-off for a rather loosely joined set of comic adventures, most critics accepted Mrs. Claffenden's third-act speech as a delivery of Crothers's attack against feminism. Typical headlines reviewing the play read: "New Play Satirizes the Advanced Girl" and "The Taliaferros Make Fun of Advanced Feminism"[33] The *New York City Press* called it "a burlesque on feminism, and particularly the Ellen Key brand of it,"[34] and the *New York Eagle* announced that Crothers satirized "the new ideas of feminine independence in marriage, with the 'trial' marriage nonsense which has grown out of it. . . ."[35] Even critics who regarded the play not as an attack against advanced thinkers but against the confusion of their ideas in incompetent minds, still betrayed their antagonism toward the New Woman. The critic for the *New York Telegram*, for example, denied that Crothers was mocking "so profound and high minded a woman as Miss Ellen Key," and argued instead that the play satirized "the distortion and misapplication" of the view of Key "in youthful, excitable, and unprepared minds," and he blamed this condition on "young women doctors of philosophy who possess that little and narrowly focused knowledge of life that is so perilous. . . ."[36]

Crothers certainly ridicules her university woman for what she sees as an unnatural and overly intellectual impracticability; but she also shows clearly that Gail's intended marriage to Peter is worthy of Victoria's attacks. Criticizing the extreme version of a new social ideal does not necessarily dictate an embrace of the faults in the old. Crothers was moved sufficiently by the critics to clarify her position on woman's progress. She denied that she was hypocritical for writing a satire on "advanced feminism" after writing several serious plays favoring woman's freedom, and she resented having to declare her allegiance: "I hope I have proved myself a natural woman's champion, the most ardent of feminists, for I certainly believe in women and their capacity to earn their daily bread in the same field and on the same footing with men. Therefore, while my new comedy is a satire on the theories involved in the advanced women I am not laughing at them but with them. . . . Surely the most militant feminist can't fail to see that if some of her radical ideas were at once adopted and acted upon they'd be very funny and would produce very chaotic results."[37]

X *Crothers's Prewar Feminism*

The forecast that Crothers was turning her back, dramatically and personally, on feminism was certainly premature. The question remains, however, whether it is correct to portray Crothers as a feminist playwright in this early phase of her career. Certainly her plays reflect an awareness of women's issues and an engagement in questions of women's progress and status; further, they focus on New Women and put their lives and concerns at the center of dramatic conflicts in a way unduplicated in the plays of any other prewar American dramatist. At the beginning of her period as a social-problem dramatist, Crothers's delight in the evolution of modern woman put her in the profeminist camp as a dramatist, while her civic activities allied her, and other activist women, by more tenuous links to the larger woman movement in America.

By the end of her social-problem period, Crothers definitely voiced disappointment with what she considered the slow pace of woman's progress and the exaggerated exultation of women's triumph. In discussing the question, "What do women think of other women?" Crothers rejected the "fashionable" perspective that women "have arrived," and insisted, instead, that "they have a long way to go."[38] She identified three groups of women: frivolous egocentrics who thought nothing at all of women's issues; actively involved women who "seem blind . . . to the immense amount she has yet to do"; and women, like herself, whose busy creative lives and whose "whole" perspective on the world prevented her from an exclusive concern with "woman and her destiny" or from working for suffrage. Crothers considered her era a time of "wonderful development for women," but she condemned "the attempt of a few extremists to exalt the wonder woman at the expense of the man."

CHAPTER 4

A Formula for Success

I Changing Directions

DURING the years surrounding America's reluctant and late
entry into the Great War, Crothers played to what Mays has
called the "innocence" of America in the prewar era. Crothers
stopped debating social problems and experimented with a
formula heavily indebted to the popular "gladness" plays—a
blend of comedy and romance welded together by sentiment.[1]
Crothers did not altogether abandon her focus on woman or her
concern for woman's progress so much as she used her women
characters in a basically conventional manner, as vehicles for
romance, as objects of men's goals, and as representatives of
stereotyped or traditional feminine qualities. Of the six plays
linked in this era by their similar themes and structures, three
have men in the central role while, in a fourth, a man shares the
lead with a woman. Although Crothers was not immediately
successful in her first two attempts, of the six plays for this era,
three were great successes and one surpassed the success of *The
Three of Us.*

The motives of this new direction were numerous. Crothers
had failed to achieve commercial success, and while she was
gaining in stature, she may have resented the tag as a "writer of
tedious, doctrinaire pieces, all about one-law-for-the-man-and-
another-for-the-woman."[2] Crothers also recognized a trend
away from the realistic social-problem play. In her opinion the
stage was leaving the "era of photographic realism" and was
entering "the new era of imagination," fired by the revolutionary
European ideas about staging, lighting, and other theater arts.[3]
Crothers considered herself part of the new era, but only
selectively. She was more conspicuous for her absence from any
of the experimental currents—such as the emergent little-

76

theater movement both before and after the war—which were to charge American drama and theater with a new dynamism. Indeed, Crothers remained firmly committed to the commercial theater, both in temperament and in technique, and she remained in a camp that was to become increasingly hostile to the anticommercial apostles of a new American theater.

One activity of this era sharply characterizes the incipient gap between avant-garde and commercial dramatists. Augustus Thomas led seventy dramatists from the Society of American Dramatists and Composers in a well-publicized attempt to collaborate on a "pot boiling experiment," and Crothers was prominent in the group.[4] By following prescribed formulas for character and action, and by supplying workmanlike dialogue, the group intended to produce a successful Broadway play. The first decision of the collaborators was to agree on the selection of the star for whom the play would be a vehicle. The group selected a current actress and fashioned a character type she was identified with—a sympathetic but ruined woman. The next task was to determine the play's "big question" or "big situation" and then create events leading up to and away from this apex. By selecting an illicit romance, surrounding it with mystery and an offstage pistol shot, the collaborators capitalized on the American fondness for a certain kind of popular entertainment.

What might have seemed innocuous or even good theater sense to the Society of American Dramatists touched off a wave of revulsion in other quarters. Thomas had previously conducted this experiment in successful play construction in Professor George Pierce Baker's playwriting class at Harvard, offering the completed scenario to any student wishing to supply the dialogue, and agreeing to help find a producer for the finished piece. Baker objected to the excessive commercialism of the scheme; the young Eugene O'Neill, a student in the class, was, reputedly, so disgusted with Thomas's proposals that he rushed out after class and drank himself into a stupor.[5] This graphic but extreme "artistic" reaction to the thrust of the commercial theater clearly reflected the widening wedge between the two concepts. For our purposes, the most serious part of the rift revolved around the questions of the place of authentic realism on the American stage and the degree to which success was measured by either the quality or the quanitty of the audience attracted to the play.

II   *Appealing to Irish Americans*

The Heart of Paddy Whack (1914), Crothers's first venture in a
purely romantic mode, lasted for only twenty-six performances
in New York and aroused little critical interest. Crothers wrote
the play for Chauncey Olcott, a popular Irish matinee idol of the
1890s who specialized in swashbuckling roles, and she consciously crafted her three-act costume romance to appeal to
Irish Americans. The play is laced with purple praise for
Ireland's beauties and with exhortations to be happy in the face
of Ireland's poverty and troubles.

Set in the 1830s in a small Irish village, the play turns about the
troublesome romance of an older guardian, played by Olcott, and
his pretty young ward, Mona. Dennis O'Malley, whose nickname
and generosity are referred to in the title of the play, has secretly
impoverished himself to supply Mona with an independent
fortune. Dennis's paternal affection changes to romantic desires
as Mona grows into an attractive woman, but, embarrassed by his
feelings, Dennis hides his love and fails to see that Mona loves
him; similarly, Mona subdues her love for Dennis and believes he
has no stronger affection for her than his fatherly devotion. As
the complications mount, Dennis believes Mona wants to marry a
rich, young, handsome suitor, and Mona assumes that Dennis will
marry a rich spinster. Money is of great concern in the play, but
the apparent conflict between love and money is really no
conflict at all, since neither of the central characters believes
that money is more important than love. Only because Crothers
has painfully stretched over three acts the revelation of mutual
love between Dennis and Mona does either lover contemplate
another, richer mate.

The action of the play, as well as the characterizations,
partake of the most conventional theatrical techniques. Mona's
character is presented with a few broad strokes: a proud Irish
beauty, she has been spoiled by Dennis's secret generosity, but
she has a sweet spirit underneath her youthful arrogance.
Dennis's character, equally clichéd, has slightly more interest. A
prototype of the "pure prince," he is so virginal that he recoils in
horror when, after chastely kissing Mona on the forehead, she
forces a more passionate kiss on the lips.

The plot is moved along by secrets and misunderstandings

having to do with love, but mainly with money. Dennis's desire to keep Mona believing in her independent wealth leads to immense problems when Dennis cannot provide proof of Mona's stocks and bonds. Dennis risks his own honor to keep up the fiction, even when Mona's prospective father-in-law accuses Dennis of wicked deeds and Mona herself becomes suspicious. Crothers brings in a *deus ex machina* to resolve the conflict however, when Dennis's uncouth but steadfast serving woman tells Mona that Dennis has supplied her fortune from his own resources, and thus heals the breach between her and Dennis. The lovers are then able to unite by the final curtain.

Their romantic union follows the general American tendency to supply happy endings, but also the specifically sentimental convention to reward characters for particular virtues. Dennis, in this case, is rewarded for unselfishness, humility, and chastity, while Mona shows a disposition to change from imperious beauty to frugal housewife, cheerfully scrimping on Dennis's pitiful finances.

In addition to the play's Old-World setting, its stereotyped characterizations, and its sentimental love story, it is imbued with an otherworldly spirit quite foreign to Crothers's earlier plays. The first characters on stage are an elfish urchin and his deaf old crone of a grandmother. Michael's songs, pipe-playing, and dream-spinning, while not by any means the bulk of the play, nevertheless contribute to its aura of fantasy. The comedy of the play reflects the comic routines of vaudeville as two sets of rustic Irish types, of the Tweedledee and Tweedledum variety, become embroiled in a controversy over the sale of a horse and supply the slapstick humor of the play as they come to Dennis for legal advice. The play is swathed in a cocoon of "tenderness" and "wistfulness," critical catchwords of the time, idealizing love relations between the sexes, and burying the social realities of sex antagonisms beneath gauzy layers of romance and sentiment.

III   *Smiling through Tears*

Crothers's second sentimental attempt, *Old Lady 31* (1916), was her first commercial success since *The Three of Us* ten years before. Widely reported as a remarkable vehicle for producing tears, and critically well received, the play ran for 160 performances in New York, had a successful tour, and in 1940 was made into a movie, *The Captain Is a Lady*. Based on a novel by Louise Forsslund, the play exemplifies the function of the sentimental formula, which was temporarily to numb the audience's awareness of its own realities. As Crothers noted at the time, she set the play in 1860, a more remote time than the setting of the novel, in order to have a costume drama, "so that the quaintness of the clothes would soften the sordidness of poverty and the gentle gingers of a removed time lend a glamor and charm which the modern moment does not hold."[6] In addition to the remote time, Crothers sets her play in rural New England to use the local color and dialect for humor and interest. Further, her old people are as exotic and theatrical as were the Irish cast of her previous play.

The action of the play centers on an elderly couple who find the golden years of their life tarnished by poverty, hard luck, and human weaknesses. Although Crothers introduces these negative aspects of life more forcefully than in *The Heart of Paddy Whack*, she does not dwell on them; she continues to train most attention to the comedy, romance, and sentiment of her formula.

Part of the comedy of the play is suggested by the title's reference to one of its central characters, Abe Rose, a crusty, proud, old former sea captain who has led a gay and spendthrift life. He and his wife are forced to seek refuge in an Old Ladies' Home, and Abe thus becomes the 31st female resident. In addition to comic characterizations of the residents, Abe's entry into the all-female world sets the comic tone of disorder and confusion. Jealousy and strife among the old people hold a satiric mirror to the general relations of men and women. For example, Abe is practically invalided by the excessive pampering and devotion he receives from the old ladies, who simply cannot control their desire to serve a man. Similarly, their inevitable jealousy is aroused and forces a minicrisis when they misinterpret Abe's attentions to a particularly attractive elderly resident. Abe flees the women, as well as his wife, Angie, for refuge among "the boys," a rather aged and mellow group of misogynists who are inspired by alcohol to encourage Abe's independence from the female sex. As they see it, "Women's all right in their own way, but when it comes to nothin' *but* women night an' day, it's kind of belittlin'. It don't keep a man up to the times like. Kind of takes away his ambition" (184).

The comedy of the play is blended successfully into the sentiment in order to produce the effect of "smiling through tears." The audience's pity is aroused in the opening scene which plays on the maudlin theme of penniless old Abe and Angie, locking the door of their little cottage, and trudging to the poor farm, a ghastly destiny familiar to American audiences through popular song and melodrama. Actually, only Abe is going to the Poor House; he has just enough money to buy Angie a place in the more prestigious Old Ladies' Home. She would rather stay with Abe, but agrees to their separation so that he can salvage some pride from his defeat. Crothers plays up the pathos of the early scene: Angie is actually bidding Abe a tearful farewell at the door of the home, prepared to suffer loneliness in her last days, when the home's residents, moved by the couple's sufferings, agree to bend the rules and permit Abe to become a resident of the home.

The play's last impression, as well as its first, is sentimental. After Abe's shortlived independence spree, he returns battered and disheveled for the sustenance of the Old Ladies' Home, and, in particular, for the strength of his faithful Angie who has, literally, kept a burning candle in the window, and accepts Abe back without reproach. The play thus expounds the familiar sentimental themes of the persistence and sanctity of marital love and the prominence of maternal feelings in good women. In an equally familiar sentimental manner, the play demonstrates that fidelity is not only highly valued in itself, but usually brings rewards. Abe and Angie are surprised by a small stock-market fortune that comes from one of Abe's old investments, and by the end of the play they return together to their beloved cottage.

Romance, the third pillar for the formula, is played both in its idealized and in its more realistic mode. The jealousies and strife of the old folks in their "love" relations are counterbalanced by the romantic subplot in which a young couple who work at the old people's home struggle in adversity and ultimately triumph in their love. Although the idealization of love is pronounced in Angie's patient devotion to Abe, Crothers introduces an ironic footnote to woman's sacrificial role in marriage. When one of the ladies criticizes Angie for treating Abe "as if he was God A'mighty" (121), she is told, "Nobody worships a man because he's worth it—but just for the comfort and pleasure of doin' it"

(121). Crothers supports traditional roles for women in love, for their familiarity rather than for any inherent inferiority in women.

The play thus typifies the successful formula and was a starring vehicle for Reginald Barlow and Emma Dunn, the central old folks. But Crothers has taken care with her dramatic structure as well as with her characterization. The play's humor, for example, is more embedded in the dramatic situation than the series of slapstick interludes of *The Heart of Paddy Whack;* characters clash because of personality and value differences, and not just because of misunderstandings or mistakes. Perhaps what serves the play best is that the sentimental themes are far better realized than in the previous play because they are played off against some less-conventional character treatments and insights, such as the ironic treatment of Abe as hero. Crothers thus provides the audience with a more sophisticated theater than a music-hall love story, but she keeps the uncomfortable truths of the audience's existence at a safe distance.

Two sentimental failures followed Crothers's success with *Old Lady 31.* Crothers adapted a popular novel by Kate Douglas Wiggins, *Mother Carey's Chickens* (1917), which folded after thirty-nine performances; and she produced a second vehicle for Chauncey Olcott, *Once Upon A Time* (1918), which closed after twenty-four performances the following season. The first play is a slight effort in which Crothers collaborated so closely with the author of the novel that she did little more than transfer into a physical setting and spoken dialogue the themes, characters, and atmosphere of Wiggins's fiction. The story recounts how an urban and fatherless family, bereft in rural New England, cheerfully turns adversity into a tool for forging character. The didactic thrust of "gladness" literature, and its uncompromising optimism, have more prominence than in other Crothers plays: the sentiment is so strong that romance and comedy are given short shrift. Critics objected to the play's manner of "spreading the syrup,"[7] and one dismissed its characters as "a flock of Pollyannas in a Plymouth Rock Atmosphere,"[8] while the critic of the *New York Times* threatened to shriek if he saw yet one more play that urged people to meet the "familiar stress of life" with a philosophy that bids them "to be rustic and be glad."[9]

Once Upon a Time, although a bigger failure, is of somewhat greater interest than the adaptation which preceded it, since it minimizes its reliance on costumes and exotic characters, after Act One, and brings in the more contemporary subject of business corruption. The play begins in a wretched desert shack somewhere in the far West, but the following two acts are set in New York, in the hustle and competition of the big, modern city.

The only character the play develops in any fullness is Terry O'Shaughnessey, played by Olcott, an open-hearted and gullible inventor who returns to New York to sell an invention that represents ten years of deprivation and doggedness, and which promises to make Terry wealthy. Terry falls victim to the larceny of the modern business world, and various friends successfully cheat him out of the fortune that a patent on his invention will bring. Terry's gullibility and lack of business sense, although they appear to be flaws, are, in fact, his heroic qualities, pitted against corruption in business and society's excessive devotion to financial success.

Neither his beloved nor his young niece becomes credible characters, but Terry's relationship to each woman emphasizes some aspect of his belief that money is secondary to human happiness. The niece is simply a staple figure of sentimental literature: a sweet innocent, victimized by fate, who recovers bravely in full view of the audience. She is struck by an auto at the most critical moment in Terry's business negotiations, but Terry stays by her bedside until she is out of danger and cheerfully loses his fortune. Mary Harrington, the object of Terry's ten-year romantic quest, never takes shape as a personality. She had rejected Terry a decade before because his financial prospects seemed so dim, and she married, instead, a rich wastrel who made her life miserable. Although he is dead when Mary and Terry meet again in New York, Mary continues to play the part of married woman; thus she and Terry mutually hide their love for a good part of the play. Mary takes a job as chaperone/companion to Terry's niece, but her main function seems to be to provide visible proof that Terry can convert someone away from materialistic values. When he asks her at the play's end, "Mary, do you still think money is the most important thing in the world?" (75), she can agree that life's value is not related to wealth, but to dreams, faith, and love. Despite the current relevance of the business theme, however, it is clearly subordinate to the sentimental theme in which human values triumph over the values of the marketplace. And the title of the play signifies Crothers's main thrust—to establish an idealized or fairy-tale atmosphere in the real world of human sorrows.

IV Revising the Formula

Perhaps the failure of three of Crothers's four formula plays prompted her to redistribute the proportions of comedy, sentiment, and romance in her formula, and to minimize elements of fantasy, without discarding it altogether. The last two plays in this period have contemporary settings and more realistic treatment of social problems, especially poverty. Crothers also draws more psychologically credible characters, and more self-conscious ones as well. They speak about their personal feelings as frequently as they make global statements about human behavior and aspirations—statements which lend Crothers's sentimental plays their tone of didactic optimism.

A *Little Journey* (1918) is a good example of the adjustments she made to the formula and the success she had with it. It ran for 252 performances, gave Estelle Winwood one of her first starring roles, and was nominated for a Pulitzer Prize. Crothers's setting and plot have little to do with fantasy. She sets her play, a three-act comedy-drama, in a railroad car journeying from east to west and, as Broun notes in his generally favorable review, "Nothing much happens for most of the play"[10] except that Crothers deftly traces the interactions of her cross-section of humanity who meet by chance on this journey and draws some excellent character sketches. The central character interaction takes place between Julie Rutherford, an eastern, city-bred, young woman, and Jim West, whose name signifies his allegiance to America's frontier values. Through the clash of their personalities and beliefs, and through the resolution of their conflicts, Crothers is able to introduce the serious subject of her drama: the state of modern American civilization. Although the Great War is never referred to directly in the play, Julie is nihilistic and hopeless—the first signs of the postwar era. Jim combats her negative social and personal perspectives by an eclectic, but basically nineteenth-century-optimistic, view of the strength of the human will to survive. By the end of the play, Jim's point of view prevails, and the couple is united in love and shared ideals.

The play's single important event is a spectacular railroad

crash. Crothers is less interested in a graphic, scenic recreation of the crash, however, and more interested in the waves of emotion—fear, shock, suspense, relief—that break from the event. The plot builds up to the mechanical catastrophe through two acts of briefly surveying the life histories of the minor characters and more fully exploring the backgrounds of Jim and Julie. The mechanical catastrophe is paralleled by Julie's spiritual crisis, and her decision to attempt suicide coincides with the crash of the railway car. In the final act we see Julie and the rest of the passengers in the wake of the crash and measure the positive changes in Julie's life outlook. The play has the quality of a parable, then, dealing with the wreckage and transformation of human civilization.

The opposition between the central characters is most important, and Crothers draws her figures credibly and carefully so that they are incapable of being summed up as types. The background of each is explored, and Julie's has more impact than Jim's, mainly because the details of her social milieu emerge from her actions and her attitudes, whereas Jim's background is revealed by a straightforward narrative to Julie.

Julie is one of the few dependent and unresourceful women Crothers has placed at the center of her dramas. Through her snobbishness, her belief in appearances, and her rigidity, Crothers presents a critical portrait of modern, urban, and sophisticated society. She has been raised by a rich aunt, in an upper-middle-class milieu, to be refined, cultured, and proud. With the loss of her aunt's fortune, Julie is cut adrift to make her own way in the world, and she is almost in a state of shock. Her background has left her without skills, and without the experience of surviving on her own. Even worse, it has left Julie afraid to try making it on her own. Thus, as a penniless, single, dependent female, she boards the train to take refuge with her brother in Montana, a bitterly humiliating prospect and one which has simultaneously depressed her spirits and raised her need to maintain appearances.

The opening scene in which Julie is bid a lengthy farewell by her eastern friends shows Crothers's abilities to satirize these socially smart but trivial people and to create brisk and glittering dialogue. Although her friends commiserate with Julie's fall in the world, they offer no real assistance. Indeed, Julie's long-term beau has found that he cannot marry Julie, on his own meager $6,000 a year, and he bemoans this fact repeatedly as he wishes her a good journey. To make matters worse, Julie's trip is marred from the beginning by the loss of her ticket, further emphasizing her dependence, her economic problems, and her lack of direction.

While Julie has been cowed by experience and rendered passive in the face of trouble, Jim also has a history of defeat, as an alcoholic, yet he takes an active and assertive stance in the face of his problems. The means by which he regains sobriety and self-respect are crucial to Crothers's antiurban bias: Jim went to Montana and worked with his hands—a cure so successful for him that he decided to dedicate the rest of his life to helping men with problems similar to his. He has established a communal work camp where alcoholics regain their dignity and sobriety through cooperative labor and a spartan regime. This communal enterprise is run according to Jim's home-spun philosophy of the brotherhood of man. Further, he believes in human flexibility, in man's capacity to survive the most drastic changes in life and still be able to put down new roots. Although he does not think of adversity as a privilege, or as a blessing, he does believe that "a good hit on the head," can make people see stars "they never knew existed" (234).

The debates between Julie and Jim, though intermittently receding into the background as the lives of the other passengers come to the fore, carry the interest of the first two acts and cover several postwar concerns.

The most prominent question that arises from the clash of values is the debate over what is civilized. Jim sees Julie as someone imprisoned by external controls of respectability and propriety, and he believes that her extreme and unquestioning obedience to social norms has squelched whatever authentic spontaneity might have existed in her. This is particularly obvious to Jim, as he observes Julie "measuring things with your same old tape measure—not really approving of yourself because you're talking to me—. . . and your *real* self has never been let loose at all" (256). For Julie, however, etiquette and tradition protect rather than imprison, and she protests that simply because she observes "good manners and good form" does not mean that her mind isn't "free" (256).

But Jim connects Julie's social refinement with her cynicism and hopelessness. He is particularly bothered by her despair because he sees in it a false and fashionable beacon as to what is civilized. As he tells Julie, "If civilization *does* produce a higher breed its highness is only tested and proven *by the way* it *lives* when *life* is hardest" (255). He tells Julie that if she lets despair get the best of her then she is obviously "not the high product" she thinks she is. Finally, he spells out the alternatives he sees awaiting Julie: she can "either . . . shrivel up into a bitter old woman—or . . . live by giving what you've got to other people" (261).

What Jim is blind to is the third alternative to either passively accepting or actively resisting life's hard blows. One can choose simply not to live. As the train progresses further west, Julie increases her resistance to Jim's arguments, and although her affection for him grows, so does her despair. Jim's strength only reinforces her own sense of impotence, and she becomes more firmly convinced that suicide is the answer. Jim tries to prevent Julie from leaping off the train but, in fact, it is the train crash at the instant of Julie's decision to die that changes her death wish into a reaffirmation of life's worth.

Crothers never precisely fixes the one source of Julie's transformation, nor, wisely, does she attempt to portray it, choosing instead to dramatize the already-changed Julie. The sudden personal confrontation with death in the train wreck seems to produce, along with her growing love for Jim, the blow on the head that pushes Julie into a new consciousness of the potential of life. Julie acts courageously after the crash, ministering to the physical and emotional needs of the surviving passengers, and the more she accomplishes for others the more she recognizes her own ability to survive as an independent person. In short, she proves Jim's prescription that the value of life can be found not in individual success but in unselfish service to others.

Crothers combats modern spiritual malaise, then, with sentimental messages and images. Julie, for example, declares that suffering and love, those twin elixirs of nineteenth-century melodrama, have brought her understanding and a conviction of life's blessings. The presence of an innocent infant, calling out what is best in human hearts, is prominent throughout the play. When the child's tubercular mother dies in the crash, Julie provides such a model of compassion and generosity that all the passengers cooperate to establish a fund for the baby's care. When Julie decides to take the baby herself, she shows she has gained the life-promoting attitudes that had been lost to her as a creature of civilized restraints.

Two features of Julie's transformation are worth noting, because they contribute to the realistic, rather than fantastic, tenor of the play, whereas fairy tales gloss over transformations. First, Julie and Jim actually discuss the change in her and even disagree about its origins, since Julie believes that Jim's "love" has transformed her, while Jim, refusing to take credit, insists that the life force merely asserted its power. Second, Crothers works the sentimental theme of love's individual transforming power into the larger metaphor that human civilization can recover from its present wreckage and be transformed into something more compassionate, more generous, and more tolerant. Not only Julie, but most of the passengers, are improved by their experience. Broun, for one, was disappointed that, because the characters were so much "better" after the crash, they were much less interesting.[11] And some critics might argue that sentimental conventions portraying the benefits of a close call with death violate psychological realities. Nevertheless, it is interesting to contrast Crothers's metaphor of the wreck with its European counterpart. The purposive, nihilistic crash of civilization envisioned in Shaw's *Heartbreak House,* for example, shows modern man broken on the rocks, courting destruction, rather than enhancing life's value.

Although criticism of the play was generally favorable, if not widely enthusiastic, the content of contemporaneous reviews displays some of the problems of using the sentimental formula or of being identified with it: that is, the formula makes content irrelevant. Thus, the serious side of Crothers's romantic relationship was overlooked, as critics commented on the comic interludes or on the progress of the romance. The significance of Julie's character, or the modern meaning in the railroad crash or the clash of beliefs, elicited no response from the critics.

V   *A Final Romance*

Crothers successfully used the sentimental format once more in the following season in *39 East* (1919), a lighthearted romance which ran for 150 performances. Despite its presumably contemporary New York setting, said to be "a few years ago," the play's coy and courtly air reminds one of Crothers's earlier costume dramas, while the story of the play is ancient: the adventures of a small-town girl in the big city. The title of the play refers to the boardinghouse where Crothers lived as an aspiring actress, and a glow of nostalgia surrounds the entire play.

The play follows the adventures of Penelope Penn, a penniless minister's daughter who has traveled to New York from the Midwest to seek a career as a choir singer in order to send money home to help her brothers go to college. Finding herself part of a glut on the choir market, Penelope has become, instead, a chorus girl. She is plagued by money problems, however, and comes perilously close to losing her virtue in the lurid traps of show business which Eugene Walter had set out definitively in *The Easiest Way* (1908). The plot follows the conventional melodramatic technique of heaping trouble upon catastrophe, until disaster is inevitable, and then averting the disaster.

Penelope faces eviction from her boardinghouse because she owes two weeks back rent; she is the subject of gossip among the roomers, who suspect that Penelope's odd working hours have more to do with vice than with her religious job; she is inveigled by the stage manager of the chorus to come to supper at his apartment to discuss an advance in salary; and, most distressing of all, she is fooled by Napoleon Gibbs, a dandyish young resident of the house, into trusting him as a harmless benefactor when, in fact, he has far less innocent motives for helping her.

In best sentimental fashion, Penelope's goodness has practical returns and transforming powers. Penelope's mean landlady becomes a watchful and sympathetic godmother; Napoleon changes from a mildly lecherous young man to a protector; and the stage manager, upon hearing the story of Penelope's working to support her brothers, bursts into tears and not only gives Penelope a salary advance but promises her a new dance number in the show.

Penelope's character is imbued with an almost magical ability to transform people, and it is interesting to see that Crothers places Penelope's strength in her wide-eyed innocence. Hers is a characterization built to please an audience's fantasy: she is idealized, elfin, feminine, full of youth, hope, and her father's religious messages which she is fond of quoting, such as "We can dignify any work by a noble purpose" (238). Penelope's

entertainment value is emphasized by a rather lengthy solo
ballet she performs in the second act, in Central Park, a dance
which Crothers hardly bothers to place within a plausible
context. Penelope is so naive and pure that she belies not only
her twenty years but any suggestion that she is really part of the
twentieth century.

Crothers characteristically bolsters her romance and sentiment with a healthy dose of comedy. In this play, the comedy
comes primarily from the exaggerated types represented at the
boardinghouse where Penelope lives. An impoverished Italian
count tries to keep up his aristocratic bearing in his threadbare
suits and talks of the culture of the Old World with a mouthful of
scrambled eggs; a rock-ribbed New England spinster expresses a
rigid code of independence and self-sufficiency which is a
marked contrast to her disapproval of Penelope; the aging
Southern Belle overdresses and sustains herself on flirtation; and
perhaps more poignantly portrayed than any other minor
characters, the Clarence twins, Sadie and Myrtle, respectably
poor, pathetically spinsterish, are the epitome of "suppressed"
individuals, and open a window briefly into the growing
American familiarity with Freudian theories. The comedy of
types, however, is largely isolated from the romantic spirit of the
play, and from its melodramatic action. Indeed, the comedy is so
superior to the rest of the play that it stands apart from it.

Beneath its overwhelming spirit of whimsy, the play contains
an element of irony and a more serious theme: the contrast
between Penelope's naive idealism and Napoleon's rather jaded
outlook, reflecting the cynicism of the modern world. At the
beginning of their acquaintance, Napoleon finds it difficult to
figure Penelope out. She continually refuses his offers to show
her a "good time," and seems unreceptive to the lures of
excitement and glamour. She is obviously out of place in the
modern environment, but Napoleon assumes she must be a New
Woman: independent, and, therefore, loose-living. In his words,
"Any girl who has the pluck to leave home to make her fortune
the way you did, has got to give up all the old dope and go in for
the new" (218).

Further, Crothers treats ironically the theme of protecting
feminine virtue—a treatment most critics ignored. When Napoleon feels remorseful for his previously callow advances toward
Penelope, he vows to protect her: "A good girl is the most

helpless thing on earth and I'm going to take care of you" (251). However, Penelope does not perceive herself as weak or needing protection; she has fears of failing in the city, but she thinks of herself as "brave as a lion" (248). Further, through her plot resolution, Crothers demonstrates the effectiveness and self-sufficiency of goodness. It obviously needs no protection at all. Nevertheless, Broun took Crothers to task for idealizing naiveté, coyness, and presumably helplessness in her drama when clearly, as president of the Stage Women's War Relief and as a director, she did not accept helplessness in woman as her "most admirable and adorable quality."[12]

VI *Transforming Human Hearts*

Despite their differences in content, the last two plays demonstrate Crothers's greater success with a formula that emphasized comedy and romance more than sentiment, and that clothed the sentiment in more contemporary dress. One sentimental convention which Crothers succeeded in flavoring with greater realism is the device of transforming human hearts, or the human propensity to change for the better. By means of such a convention, sentimental literature suggests that people are basically good since they do change for the better and allows the author to sustain a dramatic world in which the current flows strongly toward positive and happy resolutions.

The characteristic handling of this "character" change usually averts the plotted disasters and turns them into success stories. In Mary's change in *Once Upon a Time,* her new self sees happiness, rather than disgrace, in poverty, and completes the love story; in Captain Abe's change, in *Old Lady 31,* he realizes that he depends on the comforts of the world of women, and his return sets the stage for the old couple's final, great reward: their windfall inheritance. In short, the transformations in which Crothers deals keep the world the same but change people's perceptions of that world. This is most vividly dramatized by Julie's changed point of view after the crash in *A Little Journey.* Her change in perspective is the difference between life and death.

To make these changes credible to a modern audience, however, demands some shifts in traditional techniques. In the first place, the characters Crothers changes are not villains to be turned from their wickedness, but basically good people to be made better. Second, Crothers plays down or keeps offstage those moments of transformation which might tax a modern audience's credulity. In *A Little Journey,* rather than subject the actress to the difficult mimetic feat of performing a nineteenth-century change of heart, Crothers uses the shock of the crash to distract us from asking too many questions: we witness Julie's change and accept her explanation that "love" and "suffering" motivated it. Similarly, in *39 East,* we do not see the rather remarkable but plainly nineteenth-century scene in which Penelope Penn's ingenuousness and purity bring tears to the eyes of a lecherous stage manager and transform his lust into paternal protectiveness. But we are told about it, and the lesser transformations of Napoleon and the landlady serve as evidence that the power of Penelope's purity is very strong indeed.

Finally, some critical attention was paid to Crothers's originality in handling sentimental themes and subjects. Heywood Broun, for example, noted that in *Old Lady 31* Crothers improved on the conventional theatrical depiction of the aged as "saintly old women and crabby old men" by presenting the truer picture of the "sweetness of years with the acidity of age."[13] Similarly, Broun applauded the more realistic handling of the invention formula in *Once Upon a Time.* In the stereotyped formula, "nobody believes in the contrivance in the first act . . . the invention turns out to be a marvelous affair in the second act . . . and the inventor gets skinned in the third act." He praised Crothers for allowing her hero to stay "skinned right up to the final curtain."[14]

In addition to her better-balanced formula, Crothers's later dramas show several advances in the playwright's dramatic structure. *The Heart of Paddy Whack,* for example, with its set comic routines, love duets, and fantasies, gives an impression of the drama as a collection of short pieces. In *A Little Journey* and *39 East,* despite the fact that they contain more scene changes, larger casts of characters, or a greater number of complications, Crothers creates a firmer impression of unity. This is due at least partially to Crothers's strengthening ability to create scenes with minor characters that organically contribute to theme rather than function to provide comic or entertaining interludes or to forward the narrative. In her earliest Irish play, for example, its choppiness is exacerbated rather than lessened by the fact that

Dennis O'Malley figures in three-quarters of the scenes, those of central importance, those of building suspense, those of comic relief, and those of fantasy. Dennis's character is not sufficiently forceful or credible to permit his playing such a variety of roles and still make a unified impression on the audience. In the later plays of the period, the central figures do not appear in every scene, yet the dramas communicate a strong awareness of their stories through scenes that deal with other matters. In *39 East*, for example, comic and realistic scenes which portray the roomers lend nothing to the plotted main events, but they counterpoint the romance of Penelope and Napoleon, with the frustration, sadness, and human realities of lives that have not found the solace of romance or marriage.

Despite their thin content, then, Crothers's plays during the war years were valuable for sharpening her theatrical skills. Critics increasingly noted Crothers's "true touches," her ability to convey a realistic sense of life through her accuracy in scenic and stage details, in costume, decor, and acting. Her comic talent and her ability to create realistic dialogue were beginning to attract critics' notice. During these years Crothers came increasingly to oversee all aspects of producing her plays, and the last three productions of this era bear the familiar phrase: "Staged under the supervision of Miss Crothers." Eventually, Crothers became something of a champion of the profession of director, and, even more, of the playwright-director; she believed that good directors would do more for the theater than any other single force.

The fact that Crothers was a woman director in a field dominated by men did not go unnoticed, but Crothers discarded the notion that women "intuitively" would make better directors than men. Indeed, she saw the "average feminine love of detail" as a disadvantage and believed that men, to date, were more successful directors because they had a "broader eye for general effects." Finally, however, she maintained that "work has no sex ... it is a question of who can produce the most charming illusion."[15]

Illusion, indeed, was Crothers's stock in trade during these years—the illusion of simplicity in a shocking and confusing world; the illusion of "the kindness of life," as one critic called it, in the midst of highly inflammatory publicity about the barbarities of war; the illusion of "sunshine" in the knowledge of darkness. These were not "delusions," but carefully created pieces, designed, as Crothers insisted her war work was, to relieve the blues of the war.[16]

Nevertheless, Crothers's dramas of this era have passed from almost all memory. If we look to some of the more persistent dramas of the era, from high comedies, like Jesse Lynch Williams's Pulitzer Prize play, *Why Marry?* (1917), or Charlotte Cushing's seminal *Pollyanna* (1916), to Clare Kummer's farce, *Good Gracious Annabelle* (1916), or the realism of O'Neill's sea plays or Susan Glaspell's *Trifles* (1916), which have sustained critical interest or which merit close attention because they portray most sharply some qualities of the era, we must conclude that Crothers's output in these years was more significant for establishing and solidifying her reputation in the theater of her times than it was significant for marking an original signature on any of her plays.

CHAPTER 5

Playwright of the Twenties

I *American Drama Becomes Modern*

THE blossoming of postwar American theater was even more vigorous and diverse than the most optimistic of prewar predictions. O'Neill now dominates, as well as signals, the arrival of the modern era in American drama, but contemporaneous critics and drama historians recorded positive impressions of a wide variety of dramatic talent and a wide range of offerings, a "flood-like force," in Crothers's words.[1] Indeed, for the first six seasons of the new decade, from 1919-1920 to 1924-1925, the average number of new productions in New York was 198, a 50 percent increase over the average number of 134 for the previous six seasons, and the average would go as high as 230 for the six seasons of the last half of the decade.[2] In addition to the quantity, the variety of theater available to Americans was almost overwhelming. The 1920s offered extreme alternatives to the playgoer, who could choose from the aesthetic motives, experimental credo, and repertory aims of the art theater; the diversionary, formulaic, long-run aims of the commercial theater;[3] and all theatrical points in between the extremes. Although the rivalry between the art and the commercial theaters was often bitter, each had a mutual influence on the other. By the decade's end, commercial aims modified the rebellious spirit of the Provincetown Players, and diminished the distinction between the Theater Guild and any commercial producer. Nevertheless, during the decade, the art theaters set a standard of artistic seriousness that challenged all American drama and contributed a sense of excitement that made theater a lively art for large numbers of Americans.

The "floodlike force" of drama of these years defies neat categorization into either schools of playwrights or kinds of plays. Certainly the most exotic and publicized new "school" of American theater was that influenced by German expressionism and epic theater and by the postrevolutionary Russian experiments in constructivist stage design.[4] Expressionism broke the fetters of realism, both in the literary elements of drama and in all the theater arts, and provided a potentially new emotional and psychic landscape for the American dramatist. It distorted and abstracted the human personality so that character became a wholly new dramatic element; it also dissolved the well-made three- or four-act play, with its attempt to create the impression of inevitability, into loosely linked or subjectively disconnected episodes, thus freeing the drama from the unities of time and place. In combination with Freudian theory, expressionist techniques probed and magnified extreme, often-disturbed psychological states, lending themselves equally well to comedy or tragedy.

As Krutch has suggested, however, the intellectual heritage of the new American drama was all of contemporary literature. The "new dramatists" were linked mainly by a shared sense of being "modern," and a belief in playwriting as "an art . . . which might aspire to interpret contemporary life as freely, as imaginatively, and with as much originality as contemporary writing in any other form."[5] Along with the new dramatist came the new critical attitudes treating American drama as a serious art. During the next decades, most American drama, whether written for the art or for the commercial audiences, was measured against the criteria of the serious, the modern, the literary, and the experimental.

Crothers entered this new era with liabilities, the most pronounced of which was an antipathy to what was experimental and exotic. For Crothers, the small art theater was the "worst menace" to American drama. "Made up of rebellious groups . . . determined to elevate the stage," they created "false ideas about the art of the theater" by overemphasizing the importance of the literary and the erudite; by insisting that their work was too "good" for commercial managers; and by implying, consequently, that whatever the commercial managers accepted for Broadway had to be "bad."[6] In Crothers's estimation, the rebels substituted a righteous sense of mission for the required degree of professional proficiency that made theater worthwhile. Crothers was also skeptical of the new experiments in dramatic construction and staging, arguing against the use of "novelty for novelty's sake," and mocking certain design innovations, such as platforms and ramps from stage to audience, noting that great plays emerged from realism, not from experiment.[7] In addition to her own reluctance to bear the visible signs of a theater radical, Crothers was also linked in the minds of many to her sentimental wartime plays and to an older generation of playwrights from an established theater which, if anything, was an embarrassment rather than a national asset. Nevertheless, after the disappointingly brief revival of *He and She* (1920), Crothers produced three successful full-length comedies and a book of six one-act plays during the first half of the decade, all of which figure significantly in her career and made her a force to be reckoned with in the modern theater.

Crothers's postwar dramas are, for the most part, a remarkable contrast to her homespun and sentimental formula plays. Crothers's comic weapons are irony and satire, and her comic territory is the modern, urban world; rich and worldly characters; the youth rebellion and generational rifts; the erosion of prewar social barriers; the conflict between old and new standards of morality; marital breakdowns; and other intellectual and cultural fashions that were altering America's profile. Stylistically, Crothers commits herself to realism, suppressing the whimsy, fantasy, and sentiment of her formula plays, perfecting her well-made constructions, so that conflicts of ideals—rather than surprise, coincidence, or invention—complicate and forward her action.

One strong link between the eras, however, is Crothers's didacticism or, in the words of Krutch, her tendency "to preach gentle sermons."[8] Crothers, in agreement with many critics of the commercial theater, objected to the stage's consistently "frittering" away its potential force when it could preach a sermon in such a fashion "that people who have forgotten the way to churches stop and listen to it."[9]

Another link between the old playwright and the new is Crothers's consistent focus on women's lives. The women in her postwar comedies serve two general functions: they represent the problematic side of modern freedom in general, being dramatic representatives of the new era because of their great contrast with their prewar style; and they become embroiled in dilemmas specifically relevant to woman's postwar progress and freedom. Crothers deemphasizes questions about woman's nature, and about her capabilities and duties, and deals more with the question of her destiny: what would she do with her "new" freedom and rights? Would she create a more meaningful life than she had under the old limitations?

II *Freedom and the Flapper*

Crothers's first new production in the 1920s, *Nice People* (1921), was a great commercial success, running for 242 performances and introducing Tallulah Bankhead, Katherine Cornell, and Francine Larrimore in their first important roles on Broadway as three flappers.[10] It was the debut production of the newly built Klaw Theater, and it forecast Crothers's new look as a contemporary playwright. The play calls attention to itself as a commentary on postwar society, especially its youth, anticipating America's obsession with its young people in the 1920s.[11] Crothers called her first act "a bit of life in New York . . . realism with a vengeance,"[12] and from the opening scene of brash young men and aggressive young women in a Park Avenue apartment, smoking, drinking, and discussing, among other subjects, whether women's underwear was outdated, Crothers establishes her new, more sophisticated milieu among the very rich, the very modern, and the very selfish. Witty banter regularly bursts from the play, and allusions to the real world of Prohibition, the Great War, bobbed hair, Fords, movies, and Childs' Restaurant occur with the same consistency as her sentimental plays shrouded the real world.

The play follows the conversion of a rich and spoiled New York flapper, Teddy Gloucester, to a hardworking, self-reliant farmer. Teddy's initial rebellion against parental authority and restrictions on her freedom is an expression of her times, while her final rebellion against the social and economic values of her own class expresses the more persistent American ideal of self-reliance. The complications of the plot are set in motion by one of Teddy's wild schemes, which she deliberately undertakes to demonstrate that neither her father nor her aunt can restrict her freedom. Teddy makes the round of roadhouses with her boyfriend, a charming but vacuous fortune-hunter, staying out all night, and spending the next day motoring through upstate New York to the Gloucesters' remote country cottage in Westchester.

A sudden storm floods the country roads and breaks the rural electrical connection, forcing Teddy and her beau to spend a second night in the cottage. Teddy's father is outraged by her defiance and, despite Teddy's insistence that she has done nothing to be ashamed of, Mr. Gloucester says she must save her reputation by marrying her boyfriend or be cut off from the Gloucester money, power, and influence. This conflict brings Teddy face to face with the strings that really bind her: first, she needs her father's money to finance her life-style; second, as a woman, she needs to preserve a "good" reputation in order to be socially acceptable.

The greatest influence in Teddy's decision to reject her legacy as a rich man's daughter is Billy Wade, a young man from the country, whom she meets by accident. With Billy's encouragement, Teddy resists the financial and social pressures to conform to her set, and vows to establish independence. She feels unskilled and incompetent, but agrees to a partnership with Billy, farming the land around the Gloucester cottage and raising chickens. After three months of farming, Teddy has a new spirit and a new confidence in herself; she has rejected the dress, style, and behavior of a flapper, and eventually, through Billy's insistence, agrees to cut herself off entirely from her father's money, as a condition of marrying her young man.

Crothers treats her young woman heroine, before her conversion, with light satire, mocking the "novelty" of her type, and stressing what "the girl of the day" reflects about postwar woman's freedom. At the same time, Teddy becomes a credible personality, an interesting mixture of youthful strengths and excesses. As a "golden" girl, rich and sought after, she is a daring trend-setter with neither financial nor moral restrictions on her behavior. She affects a hard-boiled, cynical attitude toward romance, which came to be part of the flapper stereotype, but she is not an indifferent person. Her code of behavior rests on a belief in individual freedom, but her freedom is somewhat self-conscious and always defiant: "Do everything right before everybody's eyes—and dare them to talk" (454), she advises her more timorous female friends.

Teddy's energy and frantic pace also give her character a special quality. According to the rather metaphorical stage directions, she resembles a highly strung race horse or athlete whose reflexes for action are primed to go off a thousand times more quickly than the average individual's. At twenty, Teddy is "slender," "vibrating," "high-keyed," "alertly and intensely interested in herself," and "one of the finely bred animals of care, health, and money" (453). She stays out later, drinks more, and is ruder than most of her friends, much to their admiration. She has captured the attention of Scotty Wilbur, the charming fortune-hunter sought after by other rich young women, much to their jealousy. And she displays her wealth in her extravagant clothes, marvelous pearls, three autos, and a $24,000-a-year allowance, adding much grist to the gossip mill; finally, her father gives her an endless supply of duplicate keys to his bootleg liquor cabinet, much to her aunt's disgust. In her father's and her own opinion, Teddy is successfully riding the crest of that great American wave—popularity. To the reviewers and critics, Teddy was a delightful eye-opener: a true peep into the top drawer.

Teddy is the restless center of activities and events for the first half of the play, but carefully interlaced with the action is the theme of the new freedom. What Crothers investigates in particular is the modern phenomenon of personal freedom—not sexual freedom, or intellectual freedom, but the general freedom of the individual to reject infringements, like caution, propriety, modesty, or moderation, on the individual's appetite for adventure or experience. Of the two extreme positions forwarded in the play, the conservative view is that the new freedom is no more than an old degeneracy become socially respectable and foolishly admired, and that the credo of freedom is "the song the world is riding to the devil on" (464). The radical view is that in the casual, open, and pleasure-seeking ways of the new society lie the safety and the honesty of the new age, and those who can see only defilement and devilish doings in the pursuit of joy are "narrow" and "evil minded" (461). The clash between the two views emerges from a series of direct arguments and discussions, and from the contrast between the old and new standards. Margaret Rainsford, Teddy's middle-aged aunt, represents the prewar values, and makes a studied contrast in style and ideals to her niece. Where Teddy is preoccupied with freedom, Margaret is concerned with service and self-control. Where Teddy darts and dazzles, Margaret is stately, slow-moving, and serious. While Teddy is a champion of her generation, Margaret sees youth as mindless, selfish, lax, promiscuous, unhealthy, and abetted by an older generation too weak to protest against the false philosophy of freedom.

Critics have interpreted Margaret's harsh judgments of youth to be the author's point of view. But Margaret's character bears a closer examination before accepting that interpretation. At least part of her bitterness toward youth is because her son has died in the war, and the meaning of his dying to save civilization has been eroded into a "farce," and a "hideous, horrible useless sacrifice" (459), by the chaos, waste, and degeneracy of modern civilization, all of which Teddy epitomizes. Further, while Margaret idealizes the order of the "old" days, when modesty and decorum presumably reigned in relations between the sexes, Hubert Gloucester characterizes the past as a "bottled up age . . . when we had to sneak about all the deviltry we got into" (458). Finally, Margaret is something of a prig, as her brother-in-law charges. When Teddy explains to her aunt that "kissing doesn't mean any more now than shaking hands did when you were a girl" (461), Margaret reacts as a visitor from another country, with foreign judgments. Margaret sees only promiscuity in Teddy's behavior and indecency in her dress, but we must question the validity of her extreme charges, since they are not supported in Crothers's presentation of the young woman.

Margaret represents the idealization of the "old" authority, while Teddy and her friends, and to some extent, Teddy's father, represent the idealization of freedom. In the character of Billy Wade, Crothers attempts to synthesize the beauty and freedom of uncontaminated youth with the "vital things of character," that Margaret insists belong to no generation. Billy combines a rural background with the experience of fighting in the war; he has also spent a brief period in New York in order to find out what life was all about. When he first meets Teddy, he has a high-paying job, new city friends, and a profound ambivalence toward his new life. New York, the modern world, is both "more wonderful," and "more rotten," than he could have imagined (466). The magic and excitement are there, but so is the commercial and personal corruption. Billy knows, for example, that his firm has been cheating the government and calling its tactics "big business"; he sees the casual coupling of the young men and women of his acquaintance who say they are cynical about marriage. Despite his personal alienation from some aspects of modern life, however, he has none of Margaret's priggishness, and shares none of society's harsher requirements regarding the appearance of virtue in woman. Billy appears at the door of the Gloucester cottage on the night of the storm, a stranded motorist in need of shelter. He finds Scotty in a drunken sleep, and Teddy, rather on edge, but unlike Margaret, Mr. Gloucester, and all of Teddy's friends, he makes no negative judgment of Teddy's integrity. What he offers to Teddy in his farming plan is a constructive way to harness energy unleashed by the war, and to be free of money as the standard against which all human aspirations and energies have to be measured.

Nice People is unquestionably important in Crothers's career, but critics differ about its importance in the history of American drama. Edmund Gagey regards the play simply as one of Crothers's "typical contributions to the drama of flaming youth."[13] Flexner, however, has classified the play with other "radical departures," such as Zone Gale's *Miss Lulu Bett,* and Eugene O'Neill's *The Emperor Jones,* that signaled 1920 and 1921 as a new era in American theater, finding special significance in Crothers's questioning "the new standards and social relationships which followed the world war."[14] What Crothers has done with her new subjects of social concern is to link them with a very standard theme in American drama—the excessive valuing of wealth. By examining the youth rebellion in a moneyed environment, Crothers gives the theme fresh importance.

While the theme is strong, the dramatic structure and some characterizations tend to weaken the force and integrity of the play. Several contemporary reviewers, for example, praised the first half of the play as pointed, authentic, and impressive, but condemned the second half as illogical, as if, in the words of one disappointed critic, Crothers suddenly remembered "that she is only a commercial playwright who must keep her eye on the needs of the box office."[15] In Woollcott's opinion, Teddy's regeneration through the influence of "country air . . . work in the good, clean earth, and the love of a poor young man," was a pitifully threadbare plot resolution, also attributable to box-office concerns.[16] Finally, the play's last act is something of a disappointment, the converted Teddy lacking the insight and intelligence which marked her unconverted personality. As a consequence, Crothers seems far less interested in Teddy, and fills the final scenes with intrigues, misunderstandings, and a lovers' quarrel.

The play's weakest characterization is Billy Wade and his fortuitous appearance at the remote country cottage. Although he does not exactly rescue the heroine from a burning building, his timing inevitably recalls the old-style melodramas. Crothers tries to infuse the artificial convention with new interest, and emphasizes its unreal quality. On at least four occasions, someone remarks on the strangeness of Billy's presence. Since Crothers uses Billy to express her most important theme, however, it is difficult to be simultaneously amused by Billy's presence and impressed by his purity.

In addition to Billy's weakness Crothers has also been unsuccessful in harmonizing the light and dark tones of the play. Her satire of youth's rebellion against authority is light, emphasizing the superficiality, selfishness, and conformity of these individual freedom lovers in their dress, their speech, and their manners. The social problem of the degeneracy of "nice" young people is happily resolved as the play leaves the dominant impression that young people will work out their salvation in their own way (480).

The heavier, and more universal, problem that Crothers treats in the play, is the disparity between the illusion of freedom and the reality of it. At the beginning of the play Teddy makes as much a show of her freedom as Margaret would like a show of order. But what she thinks is her freedom is very closely bound to money and the double moral standard. Crothers gives her two traditional subjects of wealth and woman's chastity very different treatments. Teddy scorns the double standard: "Isn't it a joke? Just because I'm a girl! Scotty's strutting about in town . . . while I'm waiting here for my father to forgive me"(471). The question of wealth, however, is handled melodramatically, and Teddy's conversion away from the power of the dollar is less credible than some of the character transformations in Crothers's sentimental formula plays.

Nevertheless, those critics who felt that Teddy logically should have been consigned to an unhappy ending—presumably bored, rich, and married to a roving rotter—have dismissed the point of the play. Crothers is not suggesting that young people should be punished for their exhibitions of freedom but that they should recognize that the new freedom is largely a delusion. Crothers thus pits youth's rhetoric of liberty and individuality against a less flattering reality. In answering her critics who claimed that she contrived the happy ending for the box office,

Crothers wrote: "I am optimistic about the future of the young people whose manners nevertheless shock me. . . . I predict also that these very girls who claim independence, who want to see 'life' and go to look at its dangerous places, will recover balance. Love is by no means worn out; they will fall in love and marry."[17] Crothers predicted the change would come in five years, but the play telescopes into three months on a farm what Crothers knew would take much more time, until the flapper finally would come to regard her new freedom with a more critical eye.[18]

III   The New Woman's Freedom in Marriage

Two years later, Crothers developed an entire play around the subject of the New Woman, Twenties style, and her attitude toward love and marriage. *Mary the Third* (1923), Crothers's second important comedy of this era, is one of her most favorably received and frequently anthologized plays. Its 160 performances were far outdistanced by *Nice People's* run, but most critics praise the later play as having more substantial characterizations and better comic techniques. The play is a comedy drama, with elements of romance, set in a contemporary, conservative, and prosperous midwestern household, whose traditional props are beginning to crumble under the onslaught of its younger generation. Against a comic background of youth's fashionable iconoclasm and inflated sense of superiority, Crothers sets up a serious clash between the expectations of a woman's life, and the reality of it, particularly in the area of romance. Crothers pays close attention to the impact of love and marriage on the New Woman's freedom and observes how a forceful young woman deals with the impact in a complex, transitional society. Crothers expands the generational clash from two to three generations of women and houses her three generations of Marys, Grandmother (Mary I), Mother (Mary II) and Daughter (Mary III), under one roof. The drama's title hints at royalty, perhaps a kind of gentle mockery of woman's image of herself as ruler, but also, perhaps, a hint that the contemporary Mary, the third of three generations of women, will be free to control her romantic destiny in the combination of dignity and joy missed by her predecessors.

The plot follows the activities of Mary III and a group of her friends who plan a camping trip in order to live together in honesty, avoiding the social confines and hypocrisies of their middle-class environments, as well as the romantic fallacies of their society. Mary's particular purpose is to discover which, if either, of her two beaux, is the man she wants to marry. Despite her family's objections to the plan, Mary sneaks from her house to lead the experiment. Just as the group reaches its destination, Mary is conscience-stricken about the suffering her absence will cause her parents. To save face with her friends, she fakes an appendicitis attack and returns home in time to overhear a horrible fight between her parents, revealing that their marriage has been a failure for years. Mary's antagonism toward traditional values grows. First, she becomes a strong advocate of divorce, thrusting the necessity of this action especially on her mother. Second, she discovers that woman's economic dependence is the cause of her subjugation in marriage. She draws up a rational marriage contract with the beau of her choice which includes her prescriptions for woman's independence in marriage. The play ends, however, with the rational couple overwhelmed by romance, murmuring universal endearments. Crothers leaves us with the impression that love's essence is temporarily to enthrall reason, and that this human propensity to be fooled by love is both the glory and folly of endless generations of lovers.

The plot involves a minimum of action. The single exciting scene occurs in Act Two, Scene One, when Mary and her friends head for the country at midnight in someone's auto, and Mary dares the driver on to increasingly greater speeds. Crothers shows the signs of imaginative European staging by playing the scene on a bare stage in the dark, with only occasional flashes of light, and the tension of the actors' voices, to convey excitement. In other regards, the plot is conventionally structured, even to the cliché of having Mary and her younger brother overhear the "secret" of their parents' unhappy marriage, and to the traditional romantic curtain. What stands out about the structure of the play is Crothers's use of two historical prologues which present capsule summaries of the impure motives and questionable mores of the two older generations of women. By means of these prologues Crothers maintains an ironic perspective on the older generation's negative judgments of the third Mary. She also introduces the theme of "finding the perfect love," the romantic counterpart to her realistic melody, and the frame of her play.

The dominant characteristics of each woman of the earlier generation, though modified by time and experience, persist through the play. Mary the First, who played a seductive and imperious man-stealer in the 1870s, continues to be manipulative and flirtatious, catering to men, but always pulling the strings behind their backs, and almost reveling in masculine stupidity. She sustains the domestic fiction of dominant male/helpless female as though it were the cornerstone of civilization. Her daughter, Mary the Second, who played a jolly and sensual Gibson Girl in the 1890s, is a much more ambivalent but interesting figure. She feels trapped by propriety and mediocrity, knows that something is wrong with her life but fears to look too closely. What she had originally sought in her seemingly solid man was a permanent, safe harbor from life's changes. In fact, however, she has fled from the demands of her own flesh as well as her own spirit. Because she lacks the coyness and flirtatiousness of her mother, she achieves few "victories" over her husband, and she appears more passive and acquiescent than her daughter.

After the historical prologues, the play turns to the present, 1923, and focuses on the third Mary at the height of her young womanhood. She shares the appearance and predilection for thrills of Crothers's earlier flappers. Boyishly slender, scantily dressed, living at the top of her energy, and possibly burning her candle at both ends, "she vibrates with vitality and eagerness" (20), and often comes across as a rather lively and animated puppy, clever but comical. Like Teddy, Mary yearns to find something honest and meaningful in life, but she is a more intellectual and thoughful flapper than her wealthy predecessor, and she has, from the start, criticized society for prohibiting her openness and honesty, rather than for inhibiting her desire for excitement. The opening scene shows Mary and two of her boyfriends, but rather than suggesting dissipated youth, they seem like serious young rebels discussing the merits of the proposed camping trip and pledging to avoid the antique jealousies of rival men so as to maintain a spirit of good fellowship among all three members of the "modern" triangle. Although she mocks their youthful enthusiasm, Crothers permits Mary to discard the coy reticence and the innuendoes about sex that plagued Teddy and her friends. When confronted with her family's opposition to the camping plan, Mary openly faces their unspoken objections: "We aren't going away just so we can sleep together. We could stay right at home and do that . . ." (29). Perhaps the most significant difference between the two plays' sets of young people, however, is that Mary takes a more direct role in shaping her destiny than did Teddy. Far from requiring a catalyst to fire her soul with the will to change, Mary acts as an influence on those about her—her friends, and, most importantly, her mother.

Because the play is concerned with the clash of generations, the disagreements and debates which make up a large proportion of the play merit close attention. Crothers leaves room for minor conflicts between father and son over the use and abuse of the family car, and a major conflict between husband and wife, but the play's most trenchant observations on its subjects of love, marriage, and woman's freedom come from the intergenerational conflicts among the women.

The most interesting disagreements are the ones that shed light on the ambivalent character of Mary II, the flapper's mother, frustrated by her sense of duty to the old ways but condemning the younger generation's search for "beauty and happiness all the time" as a fruitless quest. For example, when Mary I complains that her granddaughter is in danger of being "contaminated" by the moral revolution, Mary II impatiently brushes her off: "We're *all* in danger. You're in danger of becoming a fussy old woman. I'm in danger of being swamped by the hateful ugliness of—respectable, everyday life" (26). Further, she is proud of Mary's aggressiveness and idealism: "Mary won't be taken—and she won't take. She wants something different. Something that *comes*. Something that you nor I ever had" (27). But when the young Mary argues, in her exuberantly naive way, that "free love" is the "only solution" to relations between men and women, and that her mother has missed her potential by not living "with a lot of men" (32), the second Mary dismisses her daughter as trying to be "clever" and "advanced."

In another instance, the grandmother and mother clash over the younger woman's admission that she is unhappy in her marriage, an admission which the grandmother sees as shameful: "When I was your age, it was the fashion to be happy. Women loved their husbands and appreciated their blessings. Or, if they didn't, they didn't air it from the housetops" (25). Mary II rejects the feminine principles by which her mother raised her as inapplicable to the contemporary woman. Nevertheless, she upholds the traditional insistence on women making a show of their respectability. She counsels her own daughter that society will be more impressed by the external signs of wrongdoing on the camping trip than by her interior moral code, and that her reputation will be based on what it looks like she has done, not on the kind of person she is.

The disagreements reach a climax when the three generations of women meet at the breakfast table the morning after Mary's escapade and compare the strength of each generation of woman to shape her own destiny and fulfill her own desires. Mary's father has threatened to send his daughter away to learn propriety, and the grandmother's suggestion is to wheedle and manipulate the man out of this decision. She proposes that modern women could learn a great deal about managing men from her generation, who pretended to be under a man's thumbs while, in reality, they twisted men around their fingers. For the grandmother, woman's dominance is inevitable: "There ain't a man on earth as smart as a woman if she just uses what God gave her" (90), but the "new-fangled nonsense" about women showing their intelligence has led to men's fear and to more conflicts between the sexes.

In contrast to her grandmother's conniving, Mary III insists on frankness between husband and wife because marriage is "the greatest relationship in the world" (90), and must not be defiled by the tactics of a "mistress" seducing favors from her lover. But the young woman also criticizes the dutiful and submissive role of wife which has swallowed up her mother's individual identity. She challenges that her mother has not "stood up to father and looked into his eyes . . . without . . . silly compromise because he's a man and you're a woman. The interesting side of you—as a person—you haven't given to father at all" (91).

In the clash between the three generations of women, the resolution seems to favor the youngest generation. The mother, for example, comes to accept her daughter's open ways as preferable to the shabby principle of respectability she has followed; she begins to believe she has as much right to happiness as any other person and rejects the traditional prescription that women must bear their sufferings secretly and quietly. Inspired by her daughter's idealism and fearlessness, Mary II makes her first decisive move since the courtship scene, and leaves her husband, declaring that "it's the only way to find the truth" (101).

In the second resolution of the generational clash, Mary III creates an alternative to woman's manipulative or submissive position in marriage; that is, women taking a direct hand in changing the institution of marriage because "men never will" (91). The basic change Mary proposes is an economic one, giving woman independence and dignity. As she announces to her grandmother and mother: "I shall *have* my own money. I'll *make* it. I shall live with a man beacuse I love him and only as long as I love him. I shall be able to take care of myself *and* my children if necessary . . ." (92). When Mary and her fiancé draw up a verbal marriage contract, Mary's rational influence is much in evidence. She rejects endearing phrases, insists on divorce as soon as necessary, and sees herself being "as free as though we aren't married at all" (103).

In the final moments of the play, however, reason is overpowered by romance. Mary III reverses her ideas about the necessity of divorce and urges her father to follow her mother, to reconcile their differences, and "make her know you love her." In the younger generation, Crothers reintroduces the theme of the historical prologues: the universal longing for a perfect love. Just before the curtain, Mary voices the same concerns as the generations of women before her: Will her love last forever? Will it be stronger and greater than any other love?

The comedy of the play arises from the disparity between Mary's rational search for freedom in marriage and her emotional capitulation to love. Crothers portrays marriage as a social institution which organizes relations between men and women and stabilizes the family. As a social institution, it is amenable to being improved, particularly to the influence of modern woman and her ability to be an independent, respected, and equal member of the partnership. Romance, however, is distinct from marriage, and, so the plays argues, should not be "rationalized" out of existence, expressing as it does the very persistent need of men and women for beauty and transcendence. However ephemeral, disappointing, or just plain foolish romance might look to those who have passed through it to the other side of wisdom, Crothers demonstrates wittily its central function in the hopes and dreams, if not the reality, of her American lovers.

This romantic comic vision, however, was deplored by otherwise enthusiastic critics who saw not a comic but a commercial spirit at work, pulling out the clichéd happy ending for box-office success. Ludwig Lewisohn in the *Nation*, for example, complained that the "falsely happy ending" kept the play from being one of the best American comedies ever written. He praised Mary III as "the contemporary American girl of the best type," with too much "intelligence, courage, vividness of thought and impulse [to] fling herself head foremost into the delusions of the past."[19] Lewisohn attributed the ending to a general sloppiness of postwar audiences and said Crothers was catering to "the sloth of the heart."

The weakness of the play, however, may lie in its structure rather than in the playwright's motive to avoid or attract a mass audience. Crothers does not entirely succeed in translating her comic vision of the search for freedom into a coherent dramatic action, but she improves upon *Nice People* by uniting her social thesis of woman's freedom in marriage to her social satire of the bewitching aspects of romantic love. She is, however, too successful in creating the pain of an ugly marriage breakdown to swing the play back to comedy in the younger generation; further, her romantic comedy does not blend well with the realistic settings and characterizations.

IV *Freedom for the Inner Life*

America's fascination with Freud was bound to be reflected in Crothers's postwar depiction of the nation's search for freedom, just as it was reflected in a large number of plays from the 1920s, when, according to Sievers, the influence of Freud on Broadway was most keenly felt.[20] In *Expressing Willie* (1924), Crothers satirizes fashionable devotees of Freudian therapy and jargon, and attacks the popularized and distorted theory that total release of "suppressions" or "repressions" would produce healthier individuals and a more vital society.[21] The production was an even greater commercial success than *Nice People*, running for 281 performances and, according to Cordell, was Crothers's favorite among her plays.[22] It retains some historical importance as well, for, as Quinn notes, critics who had never acknowledged Crothers before now were forced to recognize her achievement as a modern playwright.[23] As in *Nice People*,

Crothers sets a timely subject in her universal concern about the dangers of wealth. Her central figure, Willie Smith, is doubly vulnerable, as a simple person and as a newly rich man, to the success image of his times. Packaged in Freudian terminology, he finds the formula for achieving personal greatness too easy to resist. Crothers also evaluates the larger impact of Freud on society, that is, the use of Freudian theory to support the concept, as the central character says, that "absolute freedom—the expression of oneself—is the most important and developing thing in the world" (504).

The play's three acts cover a weekend party at the "ridiculously magnificent" (501) and opulently overdecorated Long Island mansion of Willie Smith, newly built as a monument to his wealth. As his name suggests, Willie is an ordinary boy from a small midwestern town who has had astounding success in the toothpaste business; he is a classic though comic model of the self-made man, with the accompanying stereotyped flaws of the nouveau riche: conspicuous consumption, vulgar taste, and a yearning to be accepted by the smart set. Willie tries to buy external proof of his status: his castle, his fleet of limousines, his stable of horses. Yet the crude, provincial, simple reminders of his background keep piercing his façade of ease and assurance. He has recently taken on what he thinks are better manners along with a new group of friends, whom Quinn has called "ultra modern people . . . who live on the outskirts of art and fashion."[24] Willie sees them through a mist of envy and ignorance as beyond materialism and indifferent to wealth: "idealists—with vision," "broad," "free," and "striving for something further than life as it's ordinarily understood" (504-506). In fact, however, Willie's new friends intend to profit from his insecurity and gullibility. By exaggerating the claims of psychoanalysis, they flatter Willie with the notion that he has "buried greatness," which they alone have sensed beneath his surface, and which they alone can call out by their various talents. Through Willie's ludicruous attempts to imitate their condescending superiority, their glittering diction, their careless bantering, and their affectations of aestheticism and spirituality, Crothers mocks the foibles of the socially elite and exaggerates Willie's grotesque pose.

The plot turns about the forces pulling Willie between new and old concepts of himself. The most seductive member of the new group, Mrs. Frances Sylvester, is an exotic and much-divorced woman, devoted to psychoanalysis, who tries to use the house party as an opportunity to seduce the millionaire into a marriage proposal. Tugging in the opposite direction, to topple Willie from the false pedestal of greatness, is his blunt and skeptical old mother, who argues that Willie's about "as great as my foot" (502), and knows his friends are making an ass out of him. Mrs. Smith dredges up another feminine guest, to entice Willie away from his new friends, but Minnie Whitcomb, Willie's old hometown sweetheart, still in love with Willie, is an awkward, inadequate music teacher, a model of introversion in an age that lauded its extroverts. She seems to offer no threat to the sleek Mrs. Sylvester, but during the weekend, as the air vibrates with discussion of inhibitions, buried powers, liberated spirits, and the truth within, Minnie catches the germ and blossoms with the truth of her own power as a musician. Through a series of comic clashes and reversals, Willie's former love for Minnie does awaken in him, and there is a familiar though brief conflict between the attractions of the sophisticated versus the homespun woman. Eventually, Willie comes to recognize Frances as a fraud, and Minnie as the ugly duckling turned into a swan, but Crothers ironically undercuts this sentimental recognition because the swan, realizing her own merits, tells Willie that her horizons have broadened beyond him.

The plot is shaped, then, by the contrasting personality changes of the central figures, Minnie and Willie, and the action builds to two important scenes of transformation in Act Two, both of which convey Crothers's comic techniques. Minnie's transformation occurs offstage. We see its beginnings at the end of Act One, when Minnie, hesitantly inspired by the talk of greatness, publicly humiliates herself by attempting to play the piano and, instead, trips, and sprawls into a mass of fear. At the beginning of Act Two, Scene One, however, she reappears as a "new" and "luminous" Minnie, sweeping past her superiors and winning them over as her admirers by an impassioned virtuoso performance at the piano at the end of the scene. She not only attracts the admiration of one of the socially smart men, but she herself is intoxicated with her freedom from fear and the power of confidence. In Minnie's inebriation Crothers plants the seeds of Willie's transformation in Act Two, Scene Two, to the truth of his ordinary self.

The plot follows Crothers's fundamental principle of dramatic construction, a basic technique of the well-made play, that dramatic "inevitability" is "carefully planted, speech by speech, scene by scene, and act by act,"[25] and that a soundly constructed play is "always climbing and advancing" so that "the end of one act always pushes into the next."[26] By making her chain of comic events as stringently logical as the events leading to a tragedy, the transformations of Minnie and Willie are not only funny but credible as well.

Timing, however, is important in maintaining the comic credibility of these changes. In Willie's transformation scene, Crothers displays a mastery of comic techniques, including pace, perfectly timed recognitions, and reversals, all of which keep the audience from inappropriate sympathy although Willie suffers pain on his dramatic awakening.

Minnie enters Willie's bedroom at night, heedless of social proprieties, in order to make Willie recognize that he is hiding behind his wealth because he is insecure about the real Willie Smith. As she explains it, in breathless haste and an exaggerated sense of mission, Willie's pose of greatness is so transparent and insubstantial that he is mocked by his friends and stands to lose the deep and spiritual Frances Sylvester, who cares only for the inner and not the outer man. Minnie builds to a pitch of fervor and conviction, only to be interrupted at the height of her harangue by the knock of another visitor at Willie's door.

In order to avoid any appearance of irregularity, Willie hastily shoves the protesting Minnie, in her plain blue bathrobe, into a closet, and opens his door to a seductively negligeed Frances, come to speak of her need to get to the truth of Willie, and to help him express himself. Willie is caught between his desire for Frances and his guilt about Minnie, and can only stumble in response to Frances's obvious come-on. At the height of Frances's seduction, Minnie, sensing that her presence inhibits Willie, announces herself by shouting and banging on the closet door, until Willie releases her. Frances, furious and humiliated, accidentally shows her loathing and contempt of Willie, before sweeping out of the room. Now Willie's eyes are truly opened and he can no longer deny Minnie's claim that his friends have fooled him; Minnie, however, is still convinced that Willie can find his buried powers, and she leaves the outraged man with a final surge of enthusiastic proposals: "You show them you're bigger than your house and more powerful than your money. There *is* greatness in you. Get it out! (She shakes him vigorously by the shoulders and hurries out)" (522).

The contrasting transformations are emphasized by the power reversal in the final act. Frances, formerly the reigning and ruthless beauty, is stumped into humiliation as Minnie insists, in her effusion of self-expression, on regaling the other guests with news of the night before, the morning after. Further, Willie's old love for Minnie has been aroused, and he wants to marry her. Minnie now has all the traditional power of woman, but she desires fame and independence. When she tries to tell Willie why she cannot marry him, she innocently echoes the language he originally used in describing his sophisticated friends: "I must be *free*. You don't understand, Willie. We speak a different language. My music—my art—my inner life don't mean anything to you" (530). As the final curtain falls, Minnie is still singing the praises of Frances Sylvester as the right woman for Willie, while Willie, equally stubborn and deaf, insists he will continue to express himself, and his "self" wants Minnie. The final sounds of the play are somewhat Pirandellian: a cacophony of disputing voices, each insisting that it has the final truth.

Reviewers were especially positive about Crothers's successful creation of an American comedy of manners, a genre which foreign critics found absent in the New World. But many commentators, like Sievers, assumed Crothers personally held the play's most conservative reaction against psychoanalysis,[27]summed up by old Mrs. Smith: "If we were all running around without any suppressions, we might as well have tails again" (527). A closer look at the play's structure, however, demonstrates that Crothers explores both the positive and negative possibilities of releasing inhibitions and fears. She was not, as Flexner claims, invalidating her premise that the cult of self-expression was ludicrous simply because Minnie was transformed by it.[28] Obviously, not everyone—and, perhaps, very few—would find within themselves what Minnie found: the fact that Minnie could free herself, however, is as important as Willie's being duped. The meaning of Minnie's change is clarified by an eccentric but sympathetic artist, one of the polished group. He argues that although "the great men," the pioneer psychoanalysts, have made a "great contribution" to human knowledge and freedom, the particular means of finding one's own power are less important than having "faith that it *can* be found. . . . That's the thing that's alive in the masses—answering the cry of humanity—the faith that Divine power *is* in us all. It's coming in many ways—through many channels—under many names" (511). Crothers clearly supports whatever is "breaking down old doubt and fear" just as she despises whatever is adding to the sum of human foolishness.

Despite the sentimental overtones of this religious allusion, it would be a misrepresentation of the play to suggest that serious debates or discussions dominate the comedy. The play shows Crothers's highest comic skills in the 1920s: crisply defined comic figures that sharpen the play's comic point; clearly distinguished comic foils, each of whose excesses illuminate the other's defects; a fine sense of comic timing. She has successfully meshed the light and dark tones of her comedy and, as one critic noted, the play was distinguished from other Crothers comedies because it was "rounded" and "complete," and every dramatic power "enlarged, intensified, perfected."[29]

V *Other Work*

Several of Crothers's one-acts, from *Six One-Act Plays,* are particularly interesting to explore, both for their observations on the subject of modern woman, and for their satirical treatment of her. The best of these one-acts take their titles from Wilde: "The Importance of Being Clothed," "The Importance of Being Nice," "The Importance of Being Married," and "The Importance of Being a Woman."[30] These four plays are loosely connected by the reappearance of or reference to certain characters, by their setting among New York's socially prominent and celebrated population, and by their overarching concern with what women were doing and thinking after the war and after the gain of suffrage. As they move toward character revelations, rather than twists of plot or examination of situations, they are underscored by a portrayal of the modern woman as a personification of modern vanity and pride.

The two most important characters are socially prominent women: Nancy Marshall is a haughtily independent, wealthy, and strong-minded activist, also known as "the busiest woman in New York"; Constancia Biddle is an idle, sophisticated lady about town. Nancy is a link with the past's strong woman, while

Constancia's morality reflects the mood of the 1920s: permissive, bemused, and antagonistic to moral preachments or pronouncements which seem hypocritical.

The topical satire of "The Importance of Being Clothed" comes in the depiction of smart ladies, smart fashions, and viciousness flashing out beneath their veneer of civility, antedating the Park Avenue Jungle in Luce's *The Women* (1936). Crothers caricatures Nancy as a political activist, disguising her lust for power under her philanthropy.[31] She has pushed her way into politics on the basis of her war work but is impervious to the currents and needs of her time. For example, Nancy's political platform asks women to be considerate of each other in order to reduce "the bitterness in the labouring classes" (19), but her excessive snobbery and her lack of consideration for the women working in the fashion shop expose the emptiness of her rhetoric. Nancy declares that American women will stop the lax morality which has degenerated the high ideals of wartime, but she selects a most revealing and fashionable gown to wear to her political rally. Perhaps the greatest damnation, however, to her political aspirations, and to other women's as well, is Constancia's response when asked how she will vote in the election. Constancia coldly informs Nancy that neither she nor the other woman candidate has her vote: "Between you and her, I'd vote for the worst man going" (19).

"The Importance of Being a Woman," is the most interesting of the series. It treats the question of whether the independent woman can resist the social and psychological pressures against her independence, or whether her vanity, insecurity, and other human frailties will prevail. By calling her an old maid, Constancia goads Nancy into a defense of her single life. Arguing that being unmarried is "probably the most distinguished thing a woman *can* be" (70), Nancy emphasizes how her independence makes her superior to most women, especially to those who were involved in activities during the war: "I haven't slipped back one inch," she brags. "Most women who sort of rose to something then have slumped into themselves again, but I've gone *on.* My life gets much fuller and wider all the time. There's not room for men" (70).

Constancia's traditional viewpoint, though stamped with a modern style, argues that all women share a common identity, which can only be completed by a man; and they share a common goal, to catch a man before youth and beauty fade. Only modern women make a show of being single, happy, and superior to their feminine destiny.

Once Constancia suceeds in arousing Nancy's jealousy, claiming that her aristocratic English suitor is interested in another woman, she then advises Nancy on provocative makeup, dress, and behavior. When her suitor calls, the wooing scene of the strong woman and the weak man satirizes the conventions of romance and the social limitations on human nature, as Nancy tries desperately to hide her strength so Sir Arthur can play the aggressive man.

After three immensely successful plays in the early half of the decade, Crothers produced two more full-length dramas, *A Lady's Virtue* (1925) and *Venus* (1927). She also served as one of the dramatists in residence in a University of Pennsylvania seminar in playwriting. One of her lectures during this time is her longest theoretical discussion of drama, "The Construction of a Play."

Unfortunately, the absence of manuscripts for either full-length play leaves gaps in our tracing of Crothers's postwar dramatic concerns and of the development of her comic techniques for portraying American manners. The omission of publication of *A Lady's Virtue* is surprising. It had a moderately successful run of 136 performances, and it was included in synopsis form in *Best Plays* for 1925-1926.[32] In this play Crothers shows that "virtue" rather than sexual freedom comes more easily to the bored and restless modern housewife, despite the much-touted sexual freedom of women, and that marriage, despite its tribulations, is preferable to the fatigue and discomfort involved in carrying on an illicit affair.

The failure to publish *Venus* seems less surprising. It folded after eight performances and was a "complete failure" in the eyes of its creator, an "intellectual" monstrosity for an "emotional" medium.[33] The play is an interesting deviation from Crothers's realistic social comedies of this era, containing a parable of a more harmonious social order through the fable of life on Venus. Although the play is set on earth, two returning aviators report on the highly egalitarian society of Venus, where beings progress in terms of increased mental or spiritual perceptions. The result is the total absence of sex antagonisms currently sundering marriages and confusing earthly society. The aviators become part of an experiment on earth whereby the difference between the sexes is meant to be chemically reduced, producing feminine attributes in males, and masculine attributes in females.

The chemical backfires, however, and "those who are preponderantly masculine turn feminine with a vengeance, and vice-versa."[34] Thus, tongue in cheek, Crothers devotes most of the play to depicting two thoroughly masculinized women who "guzzle Scotch," and "make ingenuous love," and to a man who "whimpers" over his wife's curtness, wraps himself in a shawl like Strindberg's Captain in *The Father*, and does a dance similar to Nora's, in Ibsen's *A Doll's House*. Those people most transformed by the compound are relieved to resume their normal roles, but the aviators, who naturally tend toward pure intelligence and sex equality, have been unaffected by the compound and make preparations to leave the hostile atmosphere of earth to return to Venus and to the more egalitarian and intelligent life-style of that distant planet.

Despite Crothers's new look as a dramatist in the 1920s, she does not repress her sermonizing tendencies, but the precise message she hoped to convey is a matter of debate. According to most critics, Crothers criticized modern society as a conservative, idealizing prewar values and prewar behavior. Her exposure of the emptiness of young rebels, radical philosophies, and cultural novelties is taken as a sign of her general dismay at America's heady leap into postwar freedom. A closer look at the important comedies of this era, however, has shown that the comic spirit animating the plays is neither antimodern nor antiyouth.

Similarly, our analysis of Crothers's dramatic technique challenges the judgment of Crothers as a writer of flawed high comedies. Krutch, for example, places Crothers "in a continuous American tradition as old as Royal Tyler," but argues that despite her "light touch" her plays are too definitely "problem plays" to be classed as pure comedy; too "topical" to achieve the abstraction and universality of high comedy; and too sentimental and conventional in morality to convey the properly aristocratic spirit."[35] Crothers's comedies of this era, however, overlap types and are a rather distinctive blend of comedy drama, topical satire, and, on occasion, high comedy. Her method is to compound the lighter, or more topical, social question with a dilemma that resides more permanently in human nature or in modern society, and she often combines a funny or trivial resolution of her modern dilemma with a more serious conse- quence. When she has successfully blended the light and dark tones of her comedy, as she does in *Expressing Willie*, she achieves her most coherent and satisfying comic results.

VI *Crothers's Feminism in the Twenties*

Crothers's critical portrayal of her modern women calls for a reevaluation of her label as a feminist playwright. None of Crothers's comedies of this era reflects the advanced feminist thought of her day,[36] and only briefly in *Expressing Willie* does she suggest the Greenwich Village Bohemianism which housed the era's most advanced women. Further, sexual antagonism among her young people is minimal. In Crothers's opinion, "The boy of the present day understands his girl better than anyone else—far better than her mother . . . the young man is right in sympathy with her."[37] When Crothers wants to deal with hostilities between the sexes, she must turn to the older generations in her plays.

Crothers's earlier vision of woman's freedom was connected with the hope of a more just society. The motives of altruism, philanthropy, charity, selflessness, and reform were always strongly implied in the revolutionary actions and attitudes of Crothers's early women. In the 1920s, her women are motivated by quests of self-fulfillment, self-respect, and desires to increase their own knowledge and experience. Crothers does not denigrate these quests so much as she judges them temporary and incomplete. In Crothers's opinion, the modern woman "wants . . . to enjoy her freedom, to be able to call a spade a spade if she so desires, to think her own thoughts, and have the same freedom as her brothers if she so desires, but in 99 cases out of 100 she doesn't want that freedom to its full extent." [38] While Shaw built his comedies around the single deviant in a crowd of 100, Crothers resolves her comedies on the basis of the majority. And, in her view, woman's desire for freedom would, in the majority of instances, be qualified by her vulnerability to romance, to love, and to domesticity.

Since Crothers's plays of this era deal so consistently with the New Woman's attitude toward love and marriage, it is inevitable that Crothers's personal life was used to illuminate these subjects. The fact that Crothers was unmarried, publicly independent of romantic relations with men, was given the most obvious interpretation; that is, Crothers was forced to choose between career and marriage, and her resentment toward this injustice emerges in the predicaments of her women characters.[39] Crothers's own writing, however, reveals a different sense of the alienation she felt from courtship and marriage. As a woman who was as concerned "to develop her own reasoning and mental side" as men were, Crothers's development was obviously superior, and it was this superiority, rather than her career, which inhibited marriage. In her opinion, strong and superior women had a very narrow field from which to select mates. Weaker men were out of consideration, while "superior" men had difficulties relating to "superior" women. Crothers argued that she had never found "a man who was big enough, strong enough, and intellectual enough who did not also have the vices of those great qualities. Such a man has been taught by millenniums of generously providing for his women folks that his woman should depend on him economically and mentally. The superior man will not have the superior woman—not on the superior woman's terms."[40] Crothers's personal commitment to her independence and strength is as strong in this era as it was earlier in her career; but in her New Woman of the 1920s she has portrayed a more fragile and ambivalent standard-bearer for modern woman's progress.

CHAPTER 6

Playwright of the Thirties

I Broadway and the Depression

THE political engagement of American drama in the 1930s is one of the most forceful events in the history of modern American theater. The plays emerging from this time have been variously labeled dramas of attack and dramas of social comment; their function has been defined narrowly as a weapon for the American Left in its struggles against the country's political system[1] and more broadly as a cultural response to the social and economic ills of the Great Depression and the renewed specter of war resulting from the rise of totalitarian regimes in Europe.[2] The playwrights who rose to prominence in the 1930s have been called "the new realists,"[3] and they led the advance guard by staging some of America's grimmest social problems. Their favored subjects were poverty, labor strife, working-class life, prison conditions, racial antagonisms, war, and the rise of fascism. Eventually, Broadway reflected their influence. As Goldstein notes, the new realists "sharpened the tone of Broadway drama,"[4] and by the middle of the 1930s, "the most popular and successful of the writers who had come to the fore in the prosperous twenties" had added social comment to the substance of their plays and contributed "a new drama of reasoned protest,"[5] that avoided dogmatic interpretations of America's social decay and argued the country's ills from a variety of viewpoints.

Crothers, however, as Goldstein observes, was "something of an exception."[6] Although Crothers's public response to the Depression was to organize the Stage Relief Fund in 1932 to aid needy actors, her theatrical philosophy in the face of public disaster was very much what it had been during World War I: to depend on the theater for diversion from care. Crothers called the theater "the quickest escape from ourselves into the world of imagination" and believed that "escape is more and more imperative as civilization makes life more hideous for us."[7] Thus, while most playwrights in the Depression Era at least touched on money problems in their plays, Crothers "excluded any such references from her successful comedies of manners."[8] Crothers set her plays of the 1930s, as she had in the 1920s, amidst wealth and sophistication. From the perspective of the committed theater critics of the era, Crothers, like most older-generation American playwrights, was retreating from reality in her plays.[9] Crothers was even singled out at times as an example of the commercial theater's "meretricious" glamour, and her plays were castigated as "silken cocoons"[10] that temporarily diverted people from the outside world of woe, with their "clever acting, smart dialogue, dazzling costumes and effective scenery."[11]

From the perspective of mainstream theater, however, Crothers's apolitical comedies were the norm. The Broadway audience for social plays was small. For example, from the fall of 1929 to the summer of 1935, except for productions of the Group Theater and the Theater Guild, "fewer than 30 out of hundreds of New York productions treated war, poverty, and the rise of totalitarianism."[12] Immunity to the political turmoil and economic dislocations of their time, however, does not render Crothers's characters immune to chaos and disorder in their personal lives and relations. The comedy of a society caught up in a quest for freedom in the 1920s becomes the comedy of a society attempting to live with those freedoms in the 1930s and discovering their difficulties.

Thematically Crothers continues to explore the destiny of modern woman, holding up a critical but sympathetic mirror to her flaws and foibles. Theatrically, the power of her observations often is diminished by sentimental resolutions to her women's dilemmas. Crothers's women stray from their routine or ordinary lives, seeking a meaningful purpose, or an animating spark to life, demanding the right to practice their social freedoms but often being more misled than liberated by their freedom. Unlike the straying young flappers of the 1920s, the quests of Crothers's mature women of the 1930s do not result in a higher or different life-style but in a return to their ordinary lives. Thus, the comedies of Crothers's final decade emphasize the basic values in American social life and play down its obvious flaws. The burden is placed on the individual to strengthen herself despite social decay, rather than work for revolutionary change. The obvious implication is that the accumulation of improved and strengthened individuals will result in social improvement, and the implicit message is a fear of or rejection of large-scale social or political movements as a force in human destiny.

While the themes of Crothers's last comic period reflect a more conservative comic spirit than her earlier decade, the dramatic structure and comic techniques seem more influenced by bedroom farce than by social-problem drama. Triangles, romantic intrigues, disguises, secret identities, and a consuming interest in sex, both theoretical and actual, set the tone and pace of the comedies. The manners and morals of the upper class, criticized as well as admired, are conveyed through "sprightly" dialogue and "well-turned phrases,"[13] Crothers thus contributing to the flippant wit and wisecracking brilliance of American comedy.

II   *Not Such a Gay Existence*

Let Us Be Gay (1929), although written in the 1920s, has as much in common with the plays of Crothers's last decade as it does with her comedies of freedom in the earlier era. In Kitty Brown, the central character, Crothers portrays a sexually active woman who is a member of good society and a woman who not only talks about the new morality but lives it and defends her right to do so. Crothers called the drama "a sexy play for a sexy age,"[14] but Kitty scraps her devil-may-care attitude toward sex by the end of the play and pleads for husbands and wives to restore the value of marriage by practicing sexual fidelity. In her search for firm ground, rather than for excitement, Kitty typifies Crothers's women of the 1930s. The play had a good run of 132 performances in New York, with Francine Larrimore as Kitty Brown. Quinn called its dialogue "brilliant," and praised Crothers for showing a "broader sympathy with the man's point of view in a marital relationship than she had in *He and She.*"[15]

The main action of the play is preceded by a brief historical scene during which Kitty Brown confronts her husband, Bob, with his infidelity and leaves him to get a divorce. His infidelity shatters their marriage not because Bob wants to leave her for

another woman, but because Kitty cannot bear the pain of losing
her idealization of Bob, or of herself. She has built her identity as
wife and mother, and the meaning of her whole life, on romantic
visions and on the promises of her marriage vows. Bob blames
her despair on her lack of maturity and worldliness. The other
woman, he claims, "knows her way about." If Kitty understood
"the actual honest to God truth about the man and woman
business" (8), she would quickly forgive Bob and carry on in the
recognition that, in fact, nothing has happened.

The main action of the play concerns the couple's accidental
meeting, three years later, at an elegant weekend house party,
and their determination to keep their relationship a secret from
the rest of the guests. Kitty has turned upon her girlish naiveté
by becoming a woman of the world, traveling, managing her own
fashion business, and exuding the brittle confidence of a much-
admired woman. Bob has become something of an aimless
wastrel after the divorce, taking his pleasure in casual affairs.
The two still love each other, but Kitty, especially, is afraid to be
hurt again, and Bob is aghast to discover that Kitty has had
lovers. Once Kitty and Bob reach a new agreement about the
importance of fidelity in marriage for both sexes, Kitty admits
the emptiness of her so-called "gay" existence and agrees to be
reunited with her former husband. In essence, then, the main
plot is domestic melodrama with two clear messages: first,
freedom of sexual activity does not guarantee woman's happiness; second, monogamy in marriage must be an ethical
imperative for men as well as for women.

Complicating the main action for two acts, and interlaced with
it, is a web of triangular intrigue woven by Mrs. Boucicault, the
eccentric Grande Dame who is hostess of the house party. She
wants to end what she considers a dangerous romance between
her granddaughter and the older philanderer, Bob Brown. She
has invited Kitty to "vamp" Bob, assuming the two are total
strangers. She puts them in adjoining rooms, with adjacent
balconies, and hopes that once Dierdre, the granddaughter, sees
Bob's new affair, she will break with Bob and marry her
upstanding fiancé. The plan backfires, however, because
although Dierdre assumes that Bob is interested in a new sexual
conquest, she turns on her grandmother rather than Bob. She
accuses the old woman of being hypocritical about modern
morality, chastising Dierdre for loose behavior, but inviting to

her home the kind of people that epitomize the new morality. Even when Dierdre learns from Kitty that she did not win Bob by sleeping with him, Dierdre is sufficiently upset to break with her fiancé and leave her grandmother's, driving off to an unknown destination to find herself.

The subplot, or the contrivance of all the intrigues, gives Crothers scope for high comedy, observing the behavior and exchanges of her social elites, as Kitty flirts with several of the minor male characters. Boucicault has collected a lax lot; in addition to Bob and Kitty, Dierdre and her fiancé, she has Wallace Granger, and his mistress, Madge Livingston, whose life of sin has turned to tedium; and Townley Town, a kind of seedy Restoration gallant. None of the minor characters, with the exception of Mrs. Boucicault, is of great interest. Although cleverly drawn and engaging in smart repartee, their function seems to be to supply sufficient numbers to multiply intrigues, flirtations, jealousy, and to sustain a high level of gossip.

The most important characters in the play are women, and Crothers reproduces an interesting generational range of women's lives. The oldest figure is seventy-six-year-old Mrs. Boucicault, whose name might be a reminder of that nineteenth-century master of dramatic intrigue, Dion Boucicault. Boucie has qualities of the crotchety grandmother in *Mary III*, fearing the impact on Dierdre of this "modern moral revolution," but hers is a saltier and more sophisticated character; she does not make judgments about whether the moral revolution is right, but whether it makes women happy. Her past provides the historical contrast needed to understand the predicament of contemporary women. She lived for fifty hellish years with an unfaithful husband because women then had no other acceptable remedies. She considered divorce an excellent modern phenomenon and cheered her own daughter through three of them. Now, however, the novelty of divorce has worn off, and she questions whether the social changes which have affected women's lives had been good or bad. She asks the play's pivotal question about women's happiness: "Women are getting everything they think they want not, but are they any happier than they were when they used to stay at home—with their romantic illusions—and let men fool them?" (31). But Boucie does not speak for the author; rather, she is a bemused commentator of the species of modern humans around her. As she tells Kitty, "I'd like to live another 50

years—without the bother of living—to see this thing through.
I've watched a long procession of men, women, and morals
through three generations. I'm 76 and I don't know anything"
(31).

Boucie is of the oldest generation and represents the worst of
woman's lot in the past; Dierdre represents the youngest
generation and, presumably, the best hope for woman's progress
in the future. Kitty, for example, is pleased to see Dierdre
striding fearlessly through the world of romance, and contrasts
her boldness with the dangerous idealization with which women
of her generation surrounded their amours. Dierdre's boldness,
however, is partly a pose; she needs men as much as any earlier
generation of women, and she feels sufficiently worried about
Bob's growing attraction to Kitty to get drunk. Dierdre does ask
the most important and the most modern questions in the play.
For example, when her upright fiancé insists, with all the vigor of
a prewar chauvinist, that Dierdre like all women, must be
"decent," a virgin, if she wants to be a wife and mother, Dierdre
asks, "And if a girl wants the darling boy she marries to be the
same thing—where the hell is she going to find him?" (144). She
also asks whether anything would be wrong if she had an affair
with Bob and discovered through that affair that it was Bruce
she really wanted to marry: "Why shouldn't I have Bob for a
while and marry you, too?" (145). Dierdre's questions attack the
vestigial remains of the codes men set for their women, but
Crothers does not pursue the questions logically. They either are
unanswered or interrupted by another action. The effect is to
recognize Dierdre as a young woman who has the advantage of
"such a good start" (28) in life, as Kitty claims, but who
nevertheless has difficulty establishing an appropriate code of
personal behavior.

Kitty is the most important female figure of the play, and the
most successfully drawn. Surviving her cruel awakening she has
come out a stronger, more vibrant, and sophisticated woman.
Although Bob criticizes much of Kitty's changed behavior, he
seems to find her new self more attractive than when she was
demure and domestic. Kitty acts the role of the gay and
independent woman for the first two acts of the play: mercurial,
seductive, catty, flirtatious, she refuses to take herself or anyone
else with any seriousness. Only in the odd private moment with
Bob, away from her throng of admirers, do we see the hint of
another, less chipper side of Kitty.

The importance of Kitty's character lies in its hint of a modern Tiresias, experiencing life from the perspective of the romantic, chaste, and domesticated woman, as well as from the perspective of the philandering, free-roving male. Some of the joy of her new life comes from her economic independence. As she tells Bob: "There's something about one's own money—making it and spending it—that has—I know now how a man feels—only—he takes it for granted—and it's a new thrill to me" (96). More importantly, however, Kitty's new life has also included sexual independence, such as men have always known. Although Bob feels no threat from Kitty's financial power, he does object to her right to live according to an autonomous sexual code. When he suspects that she is having an affair with one of the houseguests, he is jealous, angry, and vindictive, threatening to take their children out of Kitty's custody if, indeed, he can prove her sexual activities.

During their climactic confrontation in Act Three, when they dissect their postdivorce lives, Kitty blames Bob for her sexual activities. She tells him that, once she discovered his infidelity, she "had to get out and find out what it was all about—to see why *you* did it" (165). In this particular case, then, woman's sexual freedom, although presented as a part of the modern woman's life-style, is rooted in her disappointment with man's lack of fidelity. Sexual freedom, per se, does not condemn a woman to infamy, but neither does it necessarily enhance her life. Indeed, the play makes a strong argument for curtailing the sexual license of both sexes. The conclusions Kitty draws from her dual life experiences are exactly opposite to what Bob had suggested in the prologue; that is, Kitty would recognize the insignificance of his sexual encounters if she had broader experiences in the world. What Kitty learns is that her series of affairs as a gay woman has left her sad and lonely. She tells Bob that "marriage means just one thing—complete and absolute fidelity or it's the biggest farce on *earth*" (165).

Although the "gaiety" of the title is meant ironically by the end of the play, the drama is nevertheless predominantly a comic rendering of modern romantic relationships. The problems the play explores are resolved not by logic but by love. This becomes particularly evident when romance resolves the serious questions raised about the viability of marriage in the modern era. Bob promises Kitty that if she will remarry him, he will make their new marriage exactly what she hoped their old marriage was. The implication is that fidelity, stability, and domestic virtues will guide their relationship. Both adults recognize, however, that marriage no longer stands as a firm social institution, enjoying high regard, or as a symbol of love and devotion. Nevertheless, they assume that by making a strong commitment to their personal values, and by putting their faith in each other, not in the institution, they can immunize themselves against the stresses that have collapsed such a high proportion of modern marriages.

The tone of the play is mainly light, wry, and bemused; serious questions about monogamy compete with rumors and gossip about ongoing romances. The setting of the weekend house party confirms the predominant tone of high comedy over domestic comedy. Mrs. Boucicault's guests have nothing to do but consider their own affairs—as well as gossip about others'—and no practical or real problem intrudes on the self-concern of these people. Ostensibly, the location is California, and Dierdre has occasion to make her entrance in a shocking bathing suit, while Kitty frequently uses the balcony outside her guest room for carrying on her flirtations. However, the sense of real time and real place is suspended while we observe the habits and manners of Crothers's upper crust.

III   *Bored Housewives*

As Husbands Go (1931) deals with the themes of woman's search for self-realization and woman's sexual freedom from the point of view of middle-class rather than upper-crust women, and from a mixed sentimental and farcical point of view. The play ran for 148 performances in New York on its first run, and for 131 performances in a 1933 revival. Crothers's story is simple and sentimental. She focuses on two middle-aged American women from Dubuque, Iowa, who are traveling companions on a summer European tour. Lucile Lingard and Emmie Sykes have met and fallen in love with two European men, a young English writer, Ronald Derbyshire, and an older Continental dandy, Hippolitus Lomi, and have been rekindled with a new sense of life. They feel inspired to overthrow the domestic dullness of Iowa, and, with some trepidations, await their men in America to start a new existence. Once on American soil, however, the love relationships run into conflicts. Emmie, a widow, has a demanding teenaged daughter who tries to hinder her mother's romance; Lucile, married but childless, feels wracked by guilt and tension, trying to keep her lover's real identity a secret while she works up the courage to tell her husband she is leaving him. Before she does so, however, the European lover begins to see her more clearly in her American commonplace identity, and as his love for her wavers, Lucile's husband maneuvers him into abandoning his plan for an elopement. Crothers neatly concludes the two stories with contrasting fates: Emmie decides in favor of her new European lover and her new life; Lucile stays with her husband and her ordinary self, but both these destinies satisfy the women.

The play focuses on two aspects of modern woman's destiny: first, it examines her sexual freedom; and second, it evaluates her expectations for happiness and self-realization. Crothers pictures the middle-aged, conservative, middle-class woman against a background of European permissiveness and sophistication. Although the language surrounding the women's discussions of European sexual mores is unbearably coy and euphemistic, the main point is that Europe has provided the women with a hedonistic rather than a puritanical attitude toward sexual pleasure. The consequence of this more open environment is not a debate about woman's right to sexual freedom, but comic confusion. Both women are enthralled by the freer European atmosphere, but paralyzed by the conflict between their desires and their provincial inhibitions. Emmie worries, for example, that "I may have left *un*done things I'll be sorry for. . . . It's been so long since a man thought I could be bad—that—that I'm made over. And I don't mind telling you that I'm just as confused as I can be—over here—as to what *is* good and bad" (18).

Women's expectations for happiness and self-fulfillment are treated somewhat more seriously. Life in Iowa, as the women see it, is cozy and dull, domestic and arid, but even worse, under the social pressures of fulfilling their domestic roles, they have lost a vital sense of themselves as people, and of the world as an exciting or adventurous place. Both Lucile and Emmie want to be valued not only for what they are to husband and to child, but for what they might be to themselves. Although this theme, too, is treated comically, it causes the women real distress rather than confusion. Emmie says, "I'm darned sick of just being Peggy's mother" (19). Her new romance has helped her see that she has "individuality" and "allure," but she fears these qualities will fade when she returns to America. As for Lucile, she is convinced that, before her new love, "no one has ever known what I *might* be—and how starving I am—to *be*—what I might be" (19), and now that she has discovered a man who fathoms her deepest self, she feels fired by a new sense of life's potential and meaning.

Crothers's interest in her current social themes is somewhat perfunctory. The plot is structured more for the purpose of romantic intrigue and comic family squabbles than for the clash between the women's middle-class domestic duties and self-images, and their newly freed desires for happiness and fulfillment. The play begins with a historical prologue showing the women and their lovers in a Paris café at dawn, just before the women prepare to leave for their American homes, their lovers to follow soon. The prologue introduces most of the main characters and conflicts, and has a somewhat exotic setting, but, like the prologue of *Let Us Be Gay,* it is an addition rather than an integral part of any domestic structure, freeing Crothers from working into exposition the necessary background information. The play proper opens in Dubuque, five weeks after the prologue, and begins to set in motion the complications that will forward the action of the plot.

Crothers interweaves two triangular relationships, Emmie's taking place in the background, Lucile's in the foreground. Emmie is caught between her passion for Hippie and her renewed zest for life, and the criticism and rejection of this new man that she faces from her daughter. This conflict see-saws through three acts, first in favor of Hippie, then in favor of her daughter, until by Act Three Emmie declares for Hippie and wins her daughter's approval as well. Lucile's triangular relationship is somewhat more complex and beset by intrigues. It dominates the action of the plot, combining the classic intrigues, secret meetings, and discoveries of romantic melodrama with the low comedy of a buffoonish drunk scene. Ronald's arrival in Iowa is justified initially as a second suitor to Emmie, but Charles pierces this flimsy disguise through an awkward and sentimental discovery in Act Two, Scene One, when Louise falters while singing a love song to the assembled company, including Ronald and Charles.

Instead of confronting Lucile, Charles works out his own strategy for separating the lovers by becoming friends with the "other" man. Gaining Ronald's confidence and admiration, Charles plays on his egocentricity and his dependence, opening his eyes to the fact that the Lucile who was a magical and raving young beauty in the Paris dawn, inspiring him to great heights, is, in reality, a nice, sweet, thirty-five-year old wife who has been taken care of all her life. In the climactic drunk scene, Act Two, Scene Two, Charles gets the young writer so inebriated after a day of fishing, that Ronald forgets his appointment to take Lucile to a country-club dance. Indeed, by the end of the scene, the triangle has been broken irrevocably, but Crothers prolongs the action one more act by contriving alarm over Lucile's disappearance, by stretching out Lucile's reaction to Ronald's farewell letter, and by extending a sentimental scene of recognition as Lucile gratefully accepts Charlie and his everyday love. The play ends on a cloyingly sweet embrace, and the prospect of the midwestern family sitting down to Sunday dinner.

The plot carries nothing like the multiple intrigues or piled-up confusion of other Crothers comedies, yet there is an artificial sense of swiftness in the pace of the play, caused mainly by a good deal of stage activity, rather than action, and one critic condemned the play's "many exits and entrances . . . arranged in the wooden, arbitrary manner of another day."[16] This is not to imply that Crothers was careless with her plot, but that she manipulated it heavily, with little concern for the integrity of her themes.

Characterization in the play is also below her usual standard. In the prologue, the four lovers are conveyed through comic characterizations. Emmie is fortyish, plump, voluble, and high-pitched; Hippie is excessively suave and a stereotyped ladies' man; Lucile is starry-eyed to have found her place in the sun as a writer's muse; Ronald is elongated, tweedy, and attractively self-impressed. Once the scene shifts to Iowa, most of the comic characterizations are maintained. Lucile, however, takes on the realistic aspects of a character from domestic drama, and so does her husband, Charles. An orphaned nephew is even arbitrarily drawn into the childless couple's life as if to emphasize the reality of their domestic roles.

None of the American characters is villainous or cruel; even Peggy, and her gangly fiancé, Jake, mock Hippie's foreignness and seediness out of nothing more serious than provincial smugness. Indeed, all the characters are stamped by an almost unbelievable degree of fundamental goodness and normalcy. Moreover, if there is a hero in the comedy it is Charles Lingard, the most amiable and generous character in the play. From the perspective of the prologue, American businessmen have been chastised for putting more importance on making money than on making love. Lucile has condemned the provincialism of the "American businessman's unshakeable belief that the wide world can provide nothing better than the house and wife he already has" (64). Crothers, however, makes her businessman, as Fergusson notes, the representative of "sanity" in the play, the character with whom the audience identifies and gains a perspective for laughing at the foibles of other characters.[17]

Ultimately, the play seems to be a clear example of Crothers's superficially spicing a play with a timely subject. She begins by suggesting a substantial analysis of modern woman's freedom, but essentially the play relies on a comic portrayal of the bored housewife and Crothers conveys no point of view regarding woman's sexual freedom. Despite all their talk Lucile and Emmie have not taken the radical step in Europe. Further, Crothers simplifies the conflicts between the women's ordinary lives and their expectations for happiness. Emmie is never seriously torn between Peggy's selfish whining and the new man in her life; and the conflict for Lucile between lover and husband is minimized when Crothers makes Ronald a skunk and Charles an angel who arranges a happy destiny for his wife.

IV   The Other Woman and the Wife

When Ladies Meet (1932) overcomes almost all of the technical inadequacies of *As Husbands Go,* and is Crothers's most effective comic treatment of modern woman's sexual freedom and her expectations for happiness. She transforms the vague social problem of woman's restlessness of the previous play into a very particular dramatic conflict between woman's idealization of love and marriage and the realities of both institutions. The successful production ran for 173 performances on its first New York run, and thirteen performances in a 1933 revival. Despite some critical weariness with another play about a romantic triangle and people trying to decide "who sleeps with whom," the general reaction was delight that Crothers had combined her usual polish and ease with a strong idea and characterization, infusing a gloomy theatrical season, and an even gloomier economic season, with gaiety and vitality. The play won the Megrue Prize for Comedy, awarded for the best comedy of the season, which left its audience "a little brighter and a little more cheered up" in the middle of America's economic Depression.[18] Although the basis of the award suggests all the faults of *As Husbands Go*, Crothers avoids both the sentimental sermonizing and superficial treatment of a current subject which mar the earlier play.

Crothers bases her story on a simple romantic triangle concerning a man, his wife, and another woman, as seen from the odd angle of the "other" woman. Mary Howard is a successful and attractive novelist, single, and in her early thirties. She falls in love with her married publisher, a philandering older man named Rogers Woodruff, and, though stricken with pangs of conscience, decides to follow the morality of the day and have an affair with him. She sets up a rendezvous at the Connecticut country home of a sympathetic socialite friend, who covers Mary's real motives with a weekend house party at which editor and author will presumably talk business. At the start of the weekend, through the intrigue of Mary's jealous friend, Jimmie Lee, the editor is temporarily called away from the country retreat and the editor's wife, Claire, is brought in disguised as Jimmie's cousin. Unaware of each other's identity, the two women immediately establish a strong rapport and develop a mutual fondness and respect. When they learn each other's identity, they do not turn on each other, but on the man. The wife leaves her husband, and the writer rejects her editor, each deeply influenced by her experience of and affection for the other woman.

The plot is complicated by romantic intrigue, but the important action is the growing enlightenment of the women, not only about each other's identity, but about their own identities as well. Mary grows up and away from her romantic naiveté; Claire rejects her lonely role as keeper of her marital contract and caretaker of Rogers's ego. Further, Crothers's dramatic structure bears the marks of her usually careful craftsmanship, and some scenes are the finest she ever wrote.

Act Two, Scene Two, for example, is one of the play's most important and effective scenes, bringing Claire and Mary together to build their friendship and then bursting the moment of good feeling with the harsh realization of each woman's real identity. The same scene in *As Husbands Go*, the drunken comradeship between Charles and Ronald, is characterized by buffoonery and slapstick timing: Louise breaks in the door to find her husband and lover arm in arm and then stalks out. In *When Ladies Meet* the scene is played in a low key, the humor characterized by a painful irony. Mary and Claire talk of love and life, discovering many shared convictions. Toward the end of the scene, through a slip of Mary's tongue, Claire becomes aware that Mary is her husband's latest and most serious amour. Shortly thereafter Rogers enters Mary's room, back from the diversionary trip to town that Jimmie Lee sent him on, unaware that Claire is in the house and that his things have been removed from the room adjoining Mary's to one down the hall. Crothers's scene conveys the shock, dismay, and embarrassment of the three members of the triangle by silence and small gestures. Claire quietly introduces herself to Mary, tells Rogers she knows about the affair, and exits. Mary, tightly self-controlled, asks Rogers to explain to Claire the nature of his love for Mary, but he says he cannot do that now, and, exclaiming how awful an encounter it is for all three of them, leaves the room. The curtain falls as Mary tries to arouse the courage to knock on Claire's door, and fails.

Another example of the play's superior structure is Crothers's excellent third act. Since the conflict is not resolved in any obvious way by the *scène a faire*, Act Three brings the principles together once again, for a final exchange and a resolution. Mary and Claire accidentally meet in the early hours of the next morning, each trying to slip away; they face each other with sympathy and understanding. Once Rogers joins the pair, it becomes obvious that he cannot tell his wife, to her face, and in front of Mary, what Mary has believed was true—that their love was perfect and incomparable, and that he never felt such love for his wife. Mary then rejects him as falling too short of her ideals; and Claire walks out on her husband. The final scene is played in quiet humor, as Bridget and Mary recognize the comic dilemma of modern woman, disabused of romantic idealizations, and needing a man as much as ever.

Although the plot is straightforward and cumulative, the action of the drama is played in two keys, the real action of the characters counterpointed by the fictional action of Mary's newest novel-in-progress. The existence of the novel is felt through all the romance and intrigue sequences, as various people comment on the novel's character and themes, and reveal something about themselves in the process. First, of course, the novel reveals Mary's idealism and naiveté; it is a fictionalized account of her falling in love with Rogers, and in the novel, the lovers have been transformed by their love from just *people* "into something *fine*" (12). Mary's heroine is more daring than Mary. She refuses to discuss the subject of divorce and has lived with her married lover for a year, in order to give them both a chance to be sure that their love is stronger than the man's marriage. At the end of a year the woman arranges a meeting with the wife in order to deal with the reality of two women loving the same man, and to determine which one of them will give him up.

Out of anger, jealousy, and prudishness, Jimmie declares that Mary's heroine is unrealistically portrayed as a decent woman, because no decent woman would have an affair. Rogers objects to the reasonable and low-key confrontation between the women, arguing it would be more realistic for them to fight. He also objects to Mary's trying to impose a "higher idealism" or meaning on the love affair. As he sees it, her people have simply been caught up by something they cannot help, and his view of the affair reveals his own philandering ways. Claire questions the heroine's naiveté in agreeing to live with her man for a year, with no strings and no promises. As she puts it, "Any married woman thinks the other woman ought to know enough not to believe a married man—if he's making love to her" (109). Claire is cynical about men, disappointed in her husband, and convinced that no man is worth the cost to woman's self-respect, integrity, and independence that would be the price of the heroine's affair. But she is convinced, as Rogers is, that the wife would be incapable of having a calm discussion about the course of her life with the other woman, whom she assumes would have to be a "vile brazen slut" (144).

Crothers has built some interesting characters out of her very familiar comic materials. Bridget Duke, for example, the weekend hostess, is the middle-aged, scatterbrained socialite, but she is also the "wise fool" of the play. Of central interest, however, is Mary Howard, last in Crothers's long line of genuinely talented, assertive, independent women, seeking to shape their destinies in a mysteriously hostile world. What is

significant about Mary is her deep sense of loneliness, a
restlessness and dissatisfaction that go beyond the bored-
housewife syndrome and wake us to a new predicament in
modern woman's life. Mary has everything that a midwestern
housewife would envy: a smart apartment in a glamorous city;
social status as a "top-drawer woman"; an exciting profession,
success and publicity; independence yet abundant attention
from men. Nevertheless, her dissatisfaction is monumental. She
complains to Jimmie: "I haven't found *anything*. Except to know
that I haven't *got* anything that really *counts*. Nobody *belongs* to
me—nobody whose very existence depends on me. I am
completely and absolutely alone" (9). According to Jimmie, Mary
is too demanding, too critical and analytical, striving too much
for perfection. But Mary counters Jimmie's charges, saying,
"Loneliness is something we can't help. If nothing comes that
completes us—what can we do?" (9). In addition to her
loneliness, Mary is also distinguished by her innocence and the
wide streak of naiveté running through her sophistication and
intelligence. Presumably, from indirect analogy to Mary's
heroine, we assume that Mary is a virgin, and that her decision to
begin an affair with Rogers represents a severe break with her
traditional morality. As Claire points out, however, for someone
who has been in the world as long as Mary, she is not only
innocent but deluded about men, and for the first time in a
Crothers play, we see Mary's innocence and naiveté as deficien-
cies and not strengths in the feminine character.

Eleanor Flexner saw in Mary's character a significant expression of the dilemma of modern woman. She had inherited,
through the struggles of previous generations of women, the
"right to work on a basis of equality with men, the vote, moral as
well as economic equality, a creative existence beyond the
confines of her home. . . .," but now that she has "broken her
chains, fought with all her might and main against being
possessed, dominated, owned by anything or anybody, she cries
out herself for the possession of another human being, for
someone to 'belong' to her, someone whose very existence
depends on her."[19] Whether or not Mary shows a shrinking away
from "feminine emancipation," she certainly reflects some sense
of modern woman's disappointment in her independence. By the
same token, however, Crothers exposes the disappointment of
the married woman who, in her attempt to live by the man's code

in marriage, faces the same loneliness. Crothers has thus contributed a new dimension to the important theme of loneliness in American drama in her portrayal of the American woman of the 1930s.[20]

The tone of the play, however, never becomes somber or maudlin, because the themes are comically embedded in the action of the play. Buffoonery is limited to the exchanges of the non-English-speaking French butler, and the non-French-speaking Walter, Bridget's nervous and highly strung boyfriend. The comedy exposes woman's weakness, that is, her need for love. In Bridget's words: "When a strong, intelligent woman *at last* persuades herself that a man is *the* thing in life she wants—of course she's the biggest *fool of all!*" (144). The deepest comedy comes from the surprising outcome of the triangular tension: each woman has helped the other to reduce her dependence on the man, rather than increase, through jealousy, the other's determination to hold on to him. Claire has tarnished the golden image of Mary's affair with Rogers not only by the unpleasant facts about his selfishness and egocentricity which emerged in their general discussion about life and love with men, but also because Mary is impressed by Claire and can find no flaws in her that would cause Rogers to turn to another woman—not even herself. In turn, meeting Mary has forced Claire to see her husband's affairs from the position of the other woman, lonely, living in false hopes, courted by the man, and a decent woman rather than the "vile brazen slut" she always assumed such a creature must be.

V An Ordinary Woman Again

Crothers achieved a stunning commercial success with her last professionally produced play, *Susan and God* (1937), which had a run of 288 performances in New York.[21] She wrote other plays, and even tried them out, before she permanently retired as a playwright, but as her final impression on American drama she left a glittering Broadway production, with sets designed by Jo Mielzener, a cast crowned by Gertrude Lawrence in the lead role of Susan Trexel, and the direction entirely under Crothers's supervision. As a theatrical production, the play provided a wide target for the attacks of committed theater critics. In addition to the glamour imparted by a cast of stars, and a well-publicized

$5,000 Parisian wardrobe for Miss Lawrence,[22] the play is elegantly set in the boudoirs, terraces, and sitting rooms of country homes. It diffuses a sense of upper-class life from its outdoor sports, such as riding and tennis, and from its indoor diversions, such as formal teas and cocktail hours. It supplies charm and an inherently superior tastefulness to its privileged characters by their witty repartee, arch humor, sophisticated observations of life's problems, and an almost total avoidance of routine annoyances. Finally, the dilemma of the central character—a restless and dissatisfied modern woman—is resolved as conventionally and happily as any of Crothers's early melodramas. In the context of Crothers's dramatic development, however, and sufficiently distanced from the critical values of the 1930s, *Susan and God* merits consideration. In addition to its comic pleasures, Crothers continues to explore woman's poste-mancipation restlessness, this time in a satirical exposé of a modern religious revival.

Set very distantly, but very perceptibly, against Europe's political chaos and the threat of war hanging over England and America, *Susan and God* focuses on wealthy, spoiled thirty-five-year-old Susan Trexel, a dissatisfied wife and bored mother, who, while traveling in Europe, encounters a new evangelical religion (bearing a close resemblance to the contemporaneous Buchmanism, or Oxford Movement), which has swept up converts throughout Europe and England and is making its way to the American shore. Susan finds that the joy of her life is revived by her faith in the movement, and a sense of purpose restored by her ability to bring others closer to God. She anticipates an outlet for her abundant energies by working full time to spread the good news.

The play begins with Susan's return to America. She tries to save her friends, a rather jaded and luxury-loving group of socialites whom Susan calls "hard-boiled worldlings" (25). Quite by accident, however, Susan converts her alcoholic husband, Barrie. She had hoped to divorce him when she returned to America, but he persuades her to give him a chance to prove that he can give up alcohol and reform his life. She agrees to a summer of domesticity at their country home, with Blossom, their daughter, and although Susan enjoys this period, she continues to prepare for her final break from domestic roles, in order to assume her public role as evangelist. Eventually,

however, Susan realizes that her happiness lies in her domestic
world and that fervor for the movement has been a substitute for
God, not a recognition of a divine presence within her.

The drama is constructed almost exclusively to give Susan
Trexel center stage and an opportunity to display the many sides
of her personality. For the first act, Susan is involved in a series of
romantic intrigues among all of the minor characters, not as a
participant, or as a bemused spectator of the mating habits of the
upper class, but as a reformer of America's crumbling morality.
She attempts to save her friends and, in retaliation for what they
see as the meddling of a woman who cannot put her own life in
order, one of the posh set fakes a conversion, thus fueling Susan's
conviction that she has religious powers. For the next two acts of
the play, Susan confronts her family and herself. She attempts to
work out her personal destiny by temporarily compromising on
her real mission in the world in order to serve the personal needs
of husband and daughter.

By the final scene of the play, Barrie is so depressed by Susan's
intention to leave her family that he breaks his vow of abstinence
and goes on a two-day drinking binge. Susan mistakenly believes
that he has run off with the woman Susan has set up as a romantic
interest for Barrie, in preparation for the time when she will be
divorcing him. When Barrie does return, Susan seeks his
forgiveness, admits her religious pretensions, and promises to put
a new life together for her family by strengthening her own inner
resources.

Although the plot is carefully constructed, the two dramatic
modes of satire and domestic comedy seem to compete, with
dangerous consequences to the play's unity. On the one hand, the
main action of the comedy is to deflate Susan's religious
pretensions. Thus the play intensifies Susan's delusions of
grandeur, makes them ludicrous to the audience, and then
teaches her the hollowness of her public religious posture. On
the other hand, the main action of the domestic drama is the
conflict between Susan's desire to rid herself of an unsatisfactory
husband and to seek fame, and her latent domestic consciousness
that suggests her real responsibilities are private and familial.

What dominates the play is the character of Susan Trexel and
Crothers's satirical, yet ultimately sympathetic, portrait of her as
a legitimately restless but self-deluded woman. Fashionable,
manipulative, a flighty egomaniac, Susan struck at least one critic

as a handicap to the entire play, since he feared Crothers was unaware of how disagreeable Susan really was.[23] Nevertheless, it seems clear from the play that Crothers carefully created Susan's flaws as well as her strengths. As Crothers describes her, Susan is "a woman with so much charm that it covers most of her faults— most of the time—for most people" (14). And one character notes that Susan's excessive charm has shielded her from the discipline of life. Thus, she finds it much easier to save Humanity and to feel love for an anonymous and undemanding crowd of strangers than to survive the day-to-day calls for her patience, tact, generosity, humor, and support made by the members of her family, people whose needs and fears compete with her own. Yet Susan is superior to most of her set. She has an energetic desire to engage life that is absent in most of her idle friends.

Naive about the world's complexities, plagued by fears and loneliness, searching for visible rewards for the expenditure of her energies, Susan is a perfect target for the strong emotional current of the new religious movement. Stark Young noted, "The new cause has appealed to the best of her and the worst of her."[24] While other critics questioned the credibility of convert- ing a woman such as Susan, Young insisted that she returns from Europe an authentic believer in God. The satire of Susan does indeed intersect with the satire of the new movement, since there is such an obvious fit between Susan's particular flaws and the ease with which the new religion satisfies all her needs.

The movement's cheerful grasping at fast remedies is re- flected critically as Susan lauds her new religion as an antidote to the "poor sick unhappy world" (27). As well as being the "only thing in the world that will stop war" (27), the religion promises personal salvation in an increasingly inhuman and meaningless world where everybody is, as Susan says, "batting round trying to find something to fill up this awful emptiness" (27).

Crothers emphasizes the shallow attraction of the new religion by juxtaposing Susan's insights into the cure for modern spiritual malaise with reports of the latest lingerie fashions. Finally, Crothers ridicules the naive belief that social and class barriers will crumble before effusions of love. Susan's first meeting with a gathering of converts made an instant and positive impact. Lady Wiggam, the British founder of the movement, had invited Susan to her home, and Susan came on the defensive: "I didn't know *anybody* and I was holding my chin as high as possible and trying to be as insulting to the English as they were to me—when Lady Wiggam *herself* floated in—and we all loved each other in a *minute*" (18). Crothers is equally scathing about public confession, a fundamental practice of the cult. Susan never questions the permanence of the instantaneous transformations after confession nor does she wonder whether the exhibitionist tendencies this practice encourages might run counter to the humility it is meant to instill. Indeed, she easily abuses the practice and in her first public confession tells the crowd that she bleaches her hair. The irony is that Susan is trapped by her facile devotion to her conversion. At the end of Act One, as she works up her evangelical pitch to save the friend who is only pretending to want help, she herself is carried away by the force of her emotion, and so is her drunken husband, standing unnoticed in the doorway.

Susan's self-delusions and the pretensions of the movement are not the only targets of criticism. Crothers also is concerned to emphasize flaws in the fabric of upper class society. Ultimately, Susan's quest for religious salvation is connected directly to the unpleasant realities of her domestic life and, in particular, to the weaknesses of Barrie's alcoholic personality. Barrie uses alcohol to cover his sense of uselessness and futility at being a rich man who has lived off his inheritance, and this has marred his marriage to Susan almost from the beginning. Susan explains to her daughter that she has worked hard to fill her life with things outside her marriage and family, not because she wanted to but because she had to (98). Susan's particular problems reflect the disordered social and family life of America's top drawer. Children, like Susan's daughter, are nurtured by boarding schools and camps, and, as Susan notes, *her* daughter has had two parents living together for a longer period than most of her friends. Social relationships, empty of trust and loyalty, thrive on back-biting gossip, hypocritical shows of affection, and the replacement of love by sex. Crothers criticizes the thoughtless acceptance of these elements of modern life, just as she deflates Susan's witless conversion to the new religion. Those critics who complained that Crothers abandoned her satire for her familiar domestic narrative overlook the connection between Susan's domestic problems and the larger social disorders.[25] What does stick out from the play in a rather disjointed manner is Susan's conflict between her need for fame and her duties to her

domestic role. Crothers treats this familiar theme in a familiar
manner. Lady Wiggam gives Susan ammunition for her fight to
leave her domestic responsibilities. She has told Susan that "God
is working through you to reach thousands of souls. You mustn't
limit it to one man and one child" (130), and Susan is loathe to
resist excitement and return to "being an ordinary woman again"
(130). But although this theme has been implicit since the play's
beginning, Crothers sidesteps it by demonstrating that Susan has
neither authentic genius nor authentic mission. Barrie speaks the
play's truth when he tells her: "I don't think you know anything
about God, Susan. It's colossal nerve for you to stand up and talk
to people who do" (146). Susan finally recognizes that she has
been deluded by her conversion and that salvation is not an
externally visible, easily attained state, but the difficult and
ongoing process of internal examination and effort. She admits:
"I don't think God is something out there to pray to—I think He's
here—in us. And I don't believe He helps one bit until we dig and
dig and dig—to get the rottenness out of us" (165). This is Susan's
first insight into herself, but it is also the occasion upon which she
turns to Barrie for strength and guidance, thus reversing their
usual domestic roles by the final curtain.

The dual transformations of Susan and Barrie by the play's end
are the resolutions of domestic melodrama rather than comedy.
Susan's transformation to the level of "ordinary woman" is
achieved by the weak dramatic convention that says arousing a
woman's jealousy is a sure way to convince her that her private
life is far more important than her public life. Barrie's success in
giving up alcohol during the summer reflects the power of love
and a good woman over a man's destiny—a conventional
melodramatic theme. His transformation from a comically
pathetic bumbler to the rock to which Susan cleaves for her
support at the end of the play permits Crothers to close her play
on the sentimental tableau emphasizing the image of the strong
man and the dependent woman.

VI   *Crothers's Reputation in the Thirties*

Crothers's plays in the 1930s were reviewed extensively in
New York newspapers, in popular weekly periodicals, and in
more specialized journals.[26] Many of the favorable reviewers,
like Burns Mantle and Brooks Atkinson, had commented on

Crothers's plays for almost two decades and during the Depression Era were especially eager to praise her comedies as evidence that the best of Broadway offered a kind of elegance, glamour, and high polish which the Hollywood studios were unable to duplicate.[27] Further, critics who were shaken by the radical ferocity of America's militant playwrights, were calmed by the "wise humor," "sanity," and "wholesomeness" of Crothers's plays.

Stark Young was one of the few critics who championed the ending of *Susan and God,* calling the marital reconciliation and the reversal of character "rightly theatric,"[28] but his judgment reflects the more general critical approval of Crothers's skill in manipulating the techniques of the well-made play. In even the most ephemeral of her Thirties productions, Crothers displays a thorough knowledge of how plays work on stage before an audience. Her dialogue, as well, was almost universally acknowledged for its virtues of clarity and economy, reflecting her goal of producing "a dialogue where every word shall tell,"[29] and her desire that all speeches "get over" to the audience exactly what she intended. One critic described the dialogue as a model for all aspiring playwrights: "facile, economical, bright, apparently spontaneous, always in character, every line written to be spoken. . . ."[30] But even the reader of Crothers's plays of this era is rewarded with dialogue whose intonations and comic rhythms bring the language of the stage to echo in the reader's ear.

Crothers gathered numerous awards and honors in the 1930s. In 1930 Ida Tarbell included her in the list of "Fifty Foremost Women of the United States."[31] In 1933 *When Ladies Meet* was awarded the Megrue Prize and cited by the Theater Club as "the most outstanding play of the season." In 1937 Crothers was honored for her distinguished achievement by 500 people at the Town Hall Club, which she helped to establish in 1920. In 1938, the Theater Club cited *Susan and God* as the season's most outstanding play. One of Crothers's highest honors came in 1939 when she was selected to receive the Chi Omega National Achievement Award for 1938. Eleanor Roosevelt made the presentation at the White House, and the celebration was marked by several speeches, the most significant of which was delivered by John Mason Brown, who had both criticized and applauded Crothers's plays of the 1930s.[32]

Thus, from the point of view of official recognition, Crothers's reputation was at its highest in the 1930s. Nevertheless, there was adverse criticism of her comedies, not only from the committed theater critics but from other commentators on the drama who had less direct ideological theses to support. This devaluation of Crothers's reputation in the 1930s reflects, at least in part, the early split between the art and commercial theaters—the tendency to measure all drama against the values of the art theater, and, in the case of the 1930s, against the values of the drama of social commitment. Within this critical framework, Crothers's success at the box office was not only ignored in assessing her plays' merits, but it was thought to be a clear indicator of her plays' defects.

The adverse critics basically attack two targets: Crothers's "theatricism" and her "competence." Generally speaking, the harshest criticism comes from critics who decried the use of theater for predominantly commercial purposes and saw in Crothers's plays clear evidence that she wanted only to draw audiences and to please them. Those critics who refused to take Crothers seriously charged her plays with being superficial, devoid of convictions. She simply peddled "sentimentalities," or, as one critic described them, "conclusions gratifying to a comfortable belief in one's neighbors."[33] Even critics who were less suspicious of Crothers's motives, however, repeated the criticism of her superficiality in kinder words. Barrett Clark, for example, called Crothers "one of our three or four women dramatists who are worth their salt," and praised her because "she has never tried to be profound for the very good reason that she has nothing profound to say in the theater. . . ."[34]

Crothers's competence, the professional polish admired by her fans, also signaled to her detractors a defect in her work. There was something too easy, too well crafted in her plays to convince people that she was a serious artist at work. Harsh critics condemned Crothers's plays as "dateless formulas" composed equally of "good humor, neat dialogue, pat characterizations,"[35] while more sympathetic critics, like Mark Van Doren, although avoiding the label of "formula," argued that Crothers's plays were "ephemeral" because she was too "wise . . . she knows as much at the beginning of a play as she does at the end, and so the impression at the end is that she has done no more than work out certain details of truth."[36]

There would be an equal danger of distorting Crothers's

comedies of this era by imposing on them more substance than they have, as there is a distortion by denying them all substance or by assuming that all plays written for the commercial theater are unworthy of serious attention. Of the four comedies discussed, only *When Ladies Meet* rewards close reading today: the relationship between Mary's fictional world and her real world gives the play an ironic depth and enlightens the audience about her plight more than does the action on stage. All four comedies, however, brought to the theater of their day, and probably would still bring today, the highest degree of technical excellence—that level of excellence toward which all arts strive. To dismiss Crothers's work in the 1930s is to encourage the general devaluation of her reputation, to ignore the merits of her comic craft, and to cut short her exploration of modern woman's lonely freedom.

VII   *After the Thirties*

Although *Susan and God* remains Crothers's final contribution to American dramatic literature, Crothers continued to remain active in the theater for another decade and a half, as a producer and director and as an interested supporter of new talent in the American theater. Her plays were revived frequently by theater groups throughout the country and made into films. The onset of World War Two, however, silenced Crothers. Mounting worry over the war prevented her from writing,[37] and she turned her energies, instead, to organizing and directing the American Theater Wing, a war relief effort composed of 1200 theater women in New York City and over 2000 women in the rest of the country.[38] After the war Crothers again turned to playwriting, but although she completed scripts, no new Crothers play was mounted. *Bill Comes Back* (1945) was never produced, and Crothers halted production of *My South Window* (1950) at the outbreak of the Korean War, since she felt a production of a comedy would be inappropriate at that time.[39]

During the Thirties and for some years after, Crothers maintained a New York apartment but spent an increasing amount of time in her large, comfortable Connecticut farmhouse, which she called "Roadside." She died there in 1958 at the age of eighty.

CHAPTER 7

Crothers's Achievement

When I look back on it, I realize it is to 3 women that I owe my freedom . . . Carlotta Nielson, who liked my play; Mrs. Wheatcroft, who asked me to be coach; and Maxine Elliott, who let me in on the professional work. For a woman it is best to look to women for help; women are more daring, they are glad to take the most extraordinary chances. . . . I think I should have been longer about my destiny if I had to battle with men alone.

Rachel Crothers,
Theater Guild Magazine, May 1931.[1]

CROTHERS'S career must be viewed in two parts: first her prewar years as a social-problem playwright; second, her postwar years as a writer of social comedies. In the early part of her career, Crothers was something of a curiosity: a woman playwright who was serious, who had ideas, and who was a social rebel. The realism of Crothers's early plays was highly praised, and she must be considered an important contributor to the arrival of modern drama on the American stage. As well, she helped to create an American drama out of American materials. She set her plays in the West, in New England, in a New York boardinghouse, and in the Bedford Reformatory, and she peopled them with characters of observable American manners and motives.

Women dramatists before the war were not scarce,[2] but neither were they highly regarded. The attitude that prevailed may be summarized by Hazlitt's comment about Susanna Centlivre, whose plays, although good, were nevertheless plays written by a woman and therefore assigned to an inferior category.[3] Crothers fought against being denied serious consideration as a dramatist, or being left out of any phase of theater, because of her sex. Very early in her career, she became integrated into the production and management of her own
146

plays. She represented in the theater "woman's progress" as defined by her times: she was succeeding in "the man's world," and she achieved her early reputation at least in part because of the oddity of her success.

In the latter part of her career, when she produced almost one new comedy a season for two decades, Crothers was accorded a status that bore little direct relationship to the quality or interest of her drama. She became known as America's foremost woman dramatist, America's most longlived and productive dramatist, and, finally, her comedies were perceived as social documents rather than as particular reflections of her times, shaped by an artistic vision and style. She was known for her sophisticated dramatic milieu, her skills in writing dialogue, crafting plots, and creating a thoroughly effective theatrical production. Her plays were typically peopled by glamorous, urban, upper-class characters, most of whom had a wide streak of Main Street piety and small-town prudery that eventually emerged from beneath their cosmopolitan features.

But what can be said in greater detail of Crothers's achievement in the American theater and what sources are available for measuring that achievement? Reviewing the critical reception of Crothers's plays has been one means of shedding light on various phases of her development, progress, and success in the theater. In the long run, however, attempts to describe Crothers's achievement with reference to the mountain of clippings of newspaper and journal articles, beginning as early as 1894, are diversionary; there is more material here for a history of American critical taste or of the conventions of the commercial theater.

As a gauge to Crothers's reputation, the reviews are informative to the degree that we discover that she was ahead of most of the critics and audiences in her prewar problem plays, but lagged behind some critics and a vocal segment of the playgoing population in the 1920s and 1930s. In the scattered references to Crothers's plays in treatments of early modern American drama, her reputation is usually downplayed because the dramas she wrote for the commercial theater are measured against criteria of the art theater, and these are criteria which Crothers's dramas fail to meet.

Few critical overviews of Crothers's work are available, and those that exist either leave important chronological gaps or depend on very particular theses upon which to base an evaluation. For example, Dickinson's brief summation of Crothers condemns her feminist plays and their ideological debates as "pretentious," and praises to excess her lighthearted romances for their sentiment.[4] In Quinn's history of American drama, the author accords Crothers a chapter which he labels "the feminine criticism of life," and follows her career to the mid-1920s. He concludes, however, that Crothers is most successful when she is most "sympathetic" to the man's point of view.[5] Flexner's compact review of Crothers's work argues that the playwright's continuous focus on women is an important theme in American drama, but Flexner evaluates Crothers's later work as she does almost every established dramatist in America, as failing to come to grips with America's social reality after the First World War.[6]

The single detailed, comprehensive account of Crothers's work, Abrahamson's dissertation, is scholarly and accompanied by lengthy appendixes of plot summaries, excerpts from critical reviews, and bibliographies of further sources of criticism on each play. The dissertation does not deal with the critical problem posed by Crothers's success in the commercial theater, and settles all controversial woman questions by reference to characters whom the author unqualifiedly accepts as Crothers's mouthpieces, such as Malcolm Gaskell on woman's purity, Dr. Remington on the unnatural phenomenon of the ambitious woman, and Jimmie Lee, repeating Gaskell's belief in female chastity.[7] Yet it is precisely in answer to the two questions of Crothers's relationship to the commercial theater and to feminism that some description of her achievement might be attempted and some refinement of her reputation proposed.

The commercial stage during Crothers's career became increasingly notorious for its play doctors and their wholesale rewriting of Broadway scripts, a practice which cast doubt on the integrity of all commercial playwrights. Indeed, Crothers indirectly criticized the play doctors by condemning the pressures on the commercial writer for box-office success, noting: "The greatest crime in the commercial theater is that its work is done too fast and under the financial pressure of try-outs and other heavy overhead expenses . . . if anything is seriously wrong with the structure of a play, you know that the solution is not going to be reached while that pressure is weighing down upon it."[8] Crothers reacted angrily to the suggestion that managers influenced or compromised her scripts. On one occasion, she wrote to the editor of *Harpers Bazaar* of her outrage that "you should think any manager in the world has influenced my plays in any way whatsoever. Good, bad, or indifferent—such as they may be—they are deeply and utterly mine."[9]

Nevertheless, the most frequently stated complaint about Crothers's plays, particularly her postwar social comedies, is that they represent the model of the successful, commercial play: ostensibly timely and with substance, but in reality, superficial, either defining too simply or resolving too easily a contemporary problem that could be, or should be, rendered with more complexity. Whether Crothers's treatment of social themes is so superficial as to permanently lower her reputation needs further debate. But the debate would be conducted on clearer grounds by separating the question of superficial or overly simple social analysis from the assumption that this aspect of Crothers's dramas was a direct result of crassly commercial motives and her overriding desire to please the lowest segment of her audience.

From the available evidence, Crothers's simplicity was a deliberate choice, reached on the basis of "failed experiments," such as *Young Wisdom,* and confirmed by the disastrous *Venus,* whose appeal was too dependent upon audience intelligence. Crothers avowed that directness and clarity were the theater's highest goals, and that theater moved people through their feelings, not through cerebral exercise.[10] Indeed, Crothers wrote: "The playwright has no business to call upon his audience to wonder what he means—to weigh his dialogue with literature. A play means the objective representation of a phase of life. . . . Ibsen is the extreme—the last word in simplicity, the directness of playwriting. He has not a universal appeal because his stories—the questions of his life with which he deals—are grim dark tragedies, glimpses into horrible truths. But . . . it is his extremely simple treatment, the everyday dialogue of his living human beings which make his plays so playable."[11]

Crothers's achievement as a feminist playwright is the second issue to discuss in an assessment of her general achievement as a dramatist. Crothers pursued the theme of woman's freedom, what she called woman's odyssey,[12] for most of her career, portraying woman's adventures and tribulations in a country whose changing social and moral landscape profoundly affected woman's self-image and aspirations. Crothers's early plays challenge relations between the sexes on a personal as well as public level because her early women alter or reject their domestic roles and display a strength and ambition that contradict the presumed attributes of weakness and self-sacrifice in the feminine nature. What Crothers's later dramas portray is that woman's odyssey foundered on the rocks of fear— fear of freedom and fear of the loneliness that seemed inevitable in a world where men were not the central purpose of woman's life. Many of Crothers's later social comedies mock these fearful women, subtly, but with an unmistakable sense of authorial superiority, and they breathe an air of exasperation about the continuation of woman's struggle to freedom.

Nevertheless, woman is at the center of Crothers's dramas throughout her career. The question remains, however, whether Crothers was a "feminist" playwright. If that label means that Crothers wrote issue-oriented dramas, unequivocally supporting the wide range of feminist causes, then it would be inaccurate to call Crothers a feminist playwright.[13] From a broader perspective, Crothers's plays are so obviously concerned with the impact of the woman question on the lives and relations of her characters that any other label but feminist seems inappropriate. Certainly, in the early part of her career, Crothers was especially interested in the character of the New Woman and in some of the issues of social and moral hygiene with which many women reformers allied themselves.[14] Crothers's plays also continuously reflected the need of woman's economic independence, so that she was no longer demeaned by marriage as her only form of financial security, and so that she could regard herself as a dignified, adult, and purposeful member of the social world.

At the same time, many Crothers plays can be interpreted as arguments for a sexual status quo. They portray woman choosing to be the power behind some ordinary man; to cherish the sweetness of small domestic triumphs; to restrain her sexual desires in order to be pure for her impure man; to capitulate to the mindless swoon of romantic love; to accept even the most inadequate of marriages or mates as preferable to spinsterhood. These characters, however, seem less to argue against woman's freedom or against feminism in its broadest sense, and more to portray the reality that the New Woman had not emerged as the common type of femininity. Further, the number and frequency of domestic or capitulating women increase in Crothers's dramas after World War I, when feminism began to lose power as a movement for social change. While her women of the 1920s and 1930s are continuously entangled in the complexities of affairs and in the nets of love, one senses the author regarding this phenomenon as a fair target for comedy, a kind of reversal of the Shavian definition that love is a woman's overestimation of the difference between one man and another. Thus Crothers locates the greatest and most comic obstacle to modern woman's freedom and progress as her need for man.

No doubt, deeper probes could be sounded about the nature and expression of Crothers's feminism as it evolves through four decades of American social and theatrical history. It is clear, however, that her dramas are more closely tied to the central concerns of feminism and of modern American women than are those of her contemporaries. On the basis of her unique development of the theme of woman's odyssey and on the basis of her distinct achievement on the commercial stage, in both the early and later parts of her career, Crothers deserves regard and attention as an important contributor to the evolution of modern American drama and to the excellence of America's mainstream theater.

Notes and References

Chapter One

1. *The Biographical Record of McLean County, Illinois* (Chicago, 1899), pp. 470–72.
2. *Ibid.*, p. 471.
3. *Ibid.*, pp.471–42.
4. Biographical Publicity Release from the John Golden Corporation, Clipping File on Rachel Crothers, Theater Collection, New York Public Library; and Henry James Forman, "The Story of Rachel Crothers, America's Leading Woman Playwright," *Pictorial Review* 32 (June 1931): 56.
5. Irving I. Abrahamson, *The Career of Rachel Crothers in the American Theater,* unpublished Ph.D. dissertation, University of Chicago, 1956, p. 5.
6. Annual Catalogue, Illinois State Normal University High School, 1891, Special Collections, Illinois State University Library.
7. For examples, Crothers's award speech, reprinted for "The National Achievement Award Is Presented to Rachel Crothers," *The Eleusis of Chi Omega* 41 (September 1939): 425–32, in Special Collections, Illinois State University Library; clippings in the Rachel Crothers file, Theater Collection, New York Public Library.
8. Certificate of Graduation from the New England School of Dramatic Instruction, Boston, 1892, in Crothers Scrapbook, Special Collections, Illinois State University Library.
9. Several programs, dated 1892–1895, can be found in Crothers Scrapbook, Special Collections, Illinois State University Library.
10. Undated clipping from Boston, in Crothers Scrapbook, Special Collections, Illinois State University Library.
11. Forman, p. 56.
12. "The National Achievement Award Is Presented to Rachel Crothers," p. 429.
13. Abrahamson, p. 7.
14. "The National Achievement Award Is Presented to Rachel Crothers," p. 429.
15. Rachel Crothers, "The Producing Playwright," *The Theater Magazine* 27 (January 1918): 34.

16. "Rachel Crothers a Leading Spirit in New York's Vacation Fund Work," *Daily Bulletin,* April 20, 1913, Crothers file, Withers Public Library.

17. Alan S. Downer, *Fifty Years of American Drama 1900-1950* (Chicago, 1951), pp. 1-2.

18. Rachel Crothers, "The Construction of a Play," in *The Art of Playwriting:* Lectures Delivered at the University of Pennsylvania by Jesse Lynch Williams, Langdon Mitchell, Lord Dunsany, Gilbert Emery and Rachel Crothers; Foreword by Arthur H. Quinn, 1928, rpt. (Freeport, New York, 1967), p. 132.

19. *Ibid.*

20. Norman Hapgood, *The Stage in America 1897-1900* (New York, 1901), pp. 10-13.

21. Abrahamson, p. 8.

22. Clippings in the Rachel Crothers file, Theater Collection, New York Public Library; see also *Bloomington Daily Pantagraph,* Oct. 10, 1902, p. 2, reprinting a story from the *New York Mail and Express* on *Which Way,* another early Crothers one-act in which she took the lead role because the student actress failed to appear.

23. Sondra R. Herman, "Loving Courtship or the Marriage Market? The Ideal and Its Critics 1871-1911," *American Quarterly* 25 (May 1973): 236-42.

24. Jack Poggi, *Theater in America: The Impact of Economic Forces 1870-1967* (Ithaca, New York, 1968), pp. 252-253.

25. Rachel Crothers, "Troubles of a Playwright," *Harpers Bazaar* 45 (January 1911): 14.

26. Virginia Frame, "Women Who Have Written Successful Plays," *The Theater* 6 (October 1906): 264.

27. Poggi, pp. 249-53.

28. For the story of the Syndicate's rise and its impact, see Poggi, Chapter One, "The Theater Becomes Centralized," and Chapter Ten, pp. 245-70, "The Effects of Economic Changes in Commercial Theater." For a contemporaneous review of events and a selection of documents pertaining to the fight against the theatrical trust, see Hapgood, Chapter One, "The Syndicate."

29. "Troubles of a Playwright," p. 14.

30. Poggi, pp. 254-56.

31. *Bloomington Daily Pantagraph,* April 26, 1907, p. 5, in the Crothers file, Withers Public Library.

32. Walter Prichard Eaton, *The American Stage of Today* (Boston, 1908), p. 22.

33. *Toledo Blade,* June 15, 1907, Robinson Locke Scrapbooks, Series 2, "Laura Hall," Theater Collection, New York Public Library.

34. *Chicago News,* June 3, 1907, clipping in the Robinson Locke Scrapbooks, Series 2, "Laura Hall," Theater Collection, New York Public Library.

35. Abrahamson, p. 195.

36. Montrose J. Moses, ed., *Representative American Dramas National and Local* (Boston, 1925), p. 450.

37. John Corbin, *New York Sun*, October 18, 1906, Abrahamson Scrapbook, I, p. 5.

38. Eaton, p. 22.

39. *Ibid.*

40. There is some indication that the latter play was written earlier than the former but no accurate record of composition dates has been found.

41. Crothers, *The Art of Playwriting*, p. 120.

42. *Ibid.*, p. 121.

43. *Theater Magazine* 6 (December 1906), cited in Abrahamson, p. 304.

Chapter Two

1. Joseph Wood Krutch, *The American Drama Since 1918*, rev. ed. (New York, 1957), p. 17.

2. Crothers, "Troubles of a Playwright," p. 14.

3. William L. O'Neill, *Divorce in the Progressive Era* (New Haven, 1967), pp. 72-73.

4. *New York World*, October 6, 1908; and *New York Times*, October 6, 1908, Robinson Locke Scrapbook, No. 179, Volume 2, "Maxine Elliott," Theater Collection, New York Public Library.

5. Burns Mantle, *Chicago Tribune*, February 13, 1908, Robinson Locke Scrapbook, No. 179, Volume 2, "Maxine Elliott," Theater Collection, New York Public Library.

6. Eleanor Flexner, *American Playwrights: 1918-1938*, 1938 rpt. (Freeport, New York, 1969), p. 240.

7. Walter Prichard Eaton, *At the New Theater and Others: The American Stage, Its Problems and Performances 1908-1910* (Boston, 1910), p. 134.

8. Ada Patterson, "Woman Must Live Out Her Destiny" (Interview with Rachel Crothers), *The Theater* 40 (May 1910): 134.

9. For examples, see reviews in *Nation* 90 (February 10, 1910): 146; in Abrahamson, p. 315; and *New York Times*, February 9, 1910, in Abrahamson, p. 316.

10. *New York Daily Tribune*, February 9, 1910, Abrahamson Scrapbook, I, p. 16.

11. *Toledo Blade*, November 16, 1909, Robinson Locke Scrapbook, No. 320, Volume 2, "Mary Mannering," Theater Collection, New York Public Library.

12. For examples, see *Toledo Blade*, November 16, 1909, Robinson Locke Scrapbook, No. 320, Volume 2, "Mary Mannering," Theater

Collection, New York Public Library; and *Theater Magazine* 11 (March 1910), in Abrahamson, p. 315.

13. For example, see Arthur Hobson Quinn, *A History of the American Drama from the Civil War to the Present Day*, rev. ed. (New York, 1936), II, p. 52; and *New York Times*, February 13, 1910, Crothers file, Withers Public Library.

14. Eaton, *At the New Theater and Others*, pp. 155–56.

15. Thomas H. Dickinson, *Playwrights of the New American Theater* (New York, 1925), p. 184.

16. Quoted in Patterson, p. 136.

17. Augustus Thomas, *As a Man Thinks*, in George Pierce Baker, ed., *Modern American Plays* (New York, 1920), p. 65.

18. *Ibid.*, p. 66.

19. Augustus Thomas, *The Print of My Remembrance* (New York: Charles Scribners and Sons, 1922), p. 451.

Chapter Three

1. Undated clipping from Boston, in Crothers Scrapbook, Special Collections, Illinois State University Library.

2. Frank Chouteau Brown, "Introduction to the Drama League Series of Modern Plays," in Charles Kenyon, *Kindling* (Garden City, New York, 1914), pp. v–xii.

3. An undated manuscript in the Theater Collection, New York Public Library, entitled *The Herfords*, is longer but essentially the same as the version prepared for Quinn's anthology. Reviews of the 1911–1912 production suggest significant differences in the conflict between Tom and Ann and these will be discussed later in this chapter.

4. Undated clipping from Boston, in Crothers Scrapbook, Special Collections, Illinois State University Library.

5. "Miss Crothers's Talk Before the Drama League," *Boston Evening Transcript*, February 14, 1912, Abrahamson Scrapbook, III, p. 38.

6. *Ibid.*

7. Henry F. May, *The End of American Innocence* (New York, 1959), p. 341.

8. Strindberg's *The Father* argues the opposite point of view, that it is the man who sacrifices his identity when he takes on the role of breadwinner.

9. *Boston Transcript*, January 16, 1912, Robinson Locke Scrapbook, No. 143, "Viola Allen," Theater Collection, New York Public Library.

10. *Atlanta Constitution*, March 26, 1912, Robinson Locke Scrapbook, No. 143, "Viola Allen," Theater Collection, New York Public Library.

11. *Boston Transcript*, January 16, 1912, Robinson Locke Scrapbook, No. 143, "Viola Allen," Theater Collection, New York Public Library.

12. Interview with Viola Allen, *Boston Herald*, January 28, 1912, Robinson Locke Scrapbook, No. 143. "Viola Allen," Theater Collection, New York Public Library.

13. Heywood Broun, *New York Tribune*, February 13, 1920, Abrahamson Scrapbook, II, p. 30.

14. Burns Mantle, *New York Evening Mail*, February 13, 1920, Abrahamson Scrapbook, II, p. 37.

15. Alexander Woollcott, *New York Times*, February 13, 1920, Abrahamson Scrapbook, II, p. 31.

16. Garff B. Wilson, *Three Hundred Years of American Drama and Theater* (Englewood Cliffs, New Jersey, 1973), p. 420.

17. Jordan Y. Miller, *American Dramatic Literature: Ten Modern Plays in Historical Perspective* (New York, 1961), p. 65.

18. Yvonne B. Shafer, "The Liberated Woman in American Plays of the Past," *Players* 49 (April-May 1974): 96.

19. Quoted in Patterson, p. 134.

20. Undated clipping from Boston, in Crothers Scrapbook, Special Collections, Illinois State University Press.

21. "The Herfords," *Christian Science Monitor*, January 15, 1912, Crothers file, Withers Public Library.

22. For example, see Anne Williams's review of a revival of *He and She*, November 1973, by The Washington Area Feminist Theater, Washinton, D.C., in *Off Our Backs*, December-January 1974, p. 12. Thanks to Dr. Selma Meyerowitz for calling my attention both to the review and to the revival.

23. Edmond M. Gagey, *Revolution in American Drama* (New York, 1947), p. 15.

24. The most publicized frank play of the era was not, however, American. Brieux's *Damaged Goods* was produced by the Medical Review of Reviews in 1913 (first privately, for special matinee audiences, then publicly in the evening, becoming a commercial success). For a social historian's interpretation of this play's importance, see John C. Burnham's "The Progressive Era Revolution in American Attitudes toward Sex," *Journal of American History* 59 (March 1973): 885-908.

25. A professional company performed *Ourselves* at the Bedford State Reformatory, "Reformatory Girls See Morals Drama," *New York City Tribune*, March 12, 1913, Crothers file, Withers Public Library.

26. "What Is the Drama League Driving At?" *New York City Tribune*, December 6, 1913, Crothers file, Withers Public Library.

27. "*Ourselves* Based on Sex Question," *Morning Telegraph*, November 23, 1913, Crothers file, Withers Public Library.

28. "More Underworld Put on the Stage," *New York Herald*, November 14, 1913, Crothers file, Withers Public Library.

29. "A Week of Underworld Drama in Which Girls-Gone-Wrong Occupy the Most Prominent Positions," *New Orleans Times-Democrat*,

November 23, 1913, Crothers file, Withers Public Library.

30. Henry Albert Phillips, "Rachel Crothers Talks of her Plays," *New York Herald Tribune*, March 15, 1931, Abrahamson Scrapbook, III, p. 59.

31. *Theater Magazine* 18 (December 1913), Abrahamson, p. 322.

32. Abrahamson, p. 197.

33. Clippings in the Crothers file, Withers Public Library.

34. *New York City Press*, January 16, 1914, Abrahamson Scrapbook, I, p. 34.

35. *New York Eagle*, January 16, 1914, Abrahamson Scrapbook, I, p. 32.

36. *New York Telegram*, January 16, 1914, Abrahamson Scrapbook, I, p. 38.

37. *New York City Sun*, January 4, 1914, Abrahamson Scrapbook, I, p. 32.

38. Marguerite Mooers Marshall, "What Do Women Think of Other Women?" *New York World*, 1915, Crothers Scrapbook, Special Collections, Illinois State University Library.

Chapter Four

1. Gagey, pp. 3–5.

2. Louis Sherwin, *New York Globe and Commercial Advertiser*, November 2, 1916, Abrahamson Scrapbook, I, p. 54.

3. Rachel Crothers, "The Future of the American Stage Depends on Directors," December 3, 1916, *New York Times Magazine*, Abrahamson Scrapbook, III, p. 4.

4. "Rachel Crothers Leads Novel Drama Plan," *Bloomington Daily Pantagraph*, May 27, 1915, p. 13, Withers Public Library.

5. Reported in Mardi Valgamae, *Accelerated Grimace* (Carbondale, Ill., 1972), p. 16.

6. Rachel Crothers, "The Dramatizing Bugaboo," undated clipping, Abrahamson Scrapbook, I, p. 48.

7. Ralph Black, *New York Tribune*, September 27, 1917, Abrahamson, p. 339.

8. *New York Dramatic Mirror*, October 6, 1917, Abrahamson, pp. 339–40.

9. *New York Times*, September 26, 1917, Abrahamson, p. 340.

10. Heywood Broun, *New York Tribune*, December 27, 1918, Abrahamson, p. 346.

11. *Ibid.*

12. Heywood Broun, *New York Tribune*, April 1, 1919, Abrahamson, p. 351.

13. Heywood Broun, *New York Tribune*, October 31, 1916, Abrahamson Scrapbook, I, p. 49.
14. Heywood Broun, *New York Tribune*, April 17, 1918, Abrahamson, p. 343.
15. Crothers, "The Producing Playwright," p. 34.
16. "The Theater Women's War Work," undated reprint from the *New York Times*, Withers Public Library.

Chapter Five

1. Crothers, *The Art of Playwriting*, p. 125.
2. Poggi, Table 2, New Productions in New York City 1899-1900 to 1966-1967, p. 47.
3. For an interesting contrast, see the discussion of e. e. cummings's *Him* (1928) in Valgamae, pp. 51-55; and the discussion of Dunning and Abbott's *Broadway* (1926) in Krutch, pp. 152-55.
4. Valgamae, especially Chapter One, "The Spell of Expressionism," and Chapter Nine, "The Legacy of Expressionism."
5. Krutch, p. 11.
6. Crothers, *The Art of Playwriting*, p. 133.
7. *Ibid.*, pp. 125-26.
8. Krutch, p. 208.
9. "Turns to Stage to Mend Morals of Present Day," undated clipping, Crothers Scrapbook, Special Collections, Illinois State University Library.
10. *Nice People* was made into a film by Paramount, produced by William De Mille in 1922, according to Copyright Records, Library of Congress.
11. William L. O'Neill, ed., *The American Sexual Dilemma* (New York, 1972), p. 4.
12. "Turns to Stage to Mend Morals of Present Day."
13. Gagey, p. 188.
14. Flexner, p. 241.
15. Louis De Foe, *New York World*, March 3, 1921, Abrahamson Scrapbook, II, p. 47.
16. Alexander Woollcott, *New York Times*, March 3, 1921, Abrahamson, p. 363.
17. "Turns to Stage to Mend Morals of Present Day."
18. The next season, Crothers again focused on a romance between two young people as the means of restoring value to a superficial and competitive world, but *Everyday* (1921), despite Tallulah Bankhead in the lead role, failed after thirty performances.
19. Ludwig Lewisohn, *Nation* 141 (March 7, 1923), in Abrahamson, p. 369.

20. W. David Sievers, *Freud on Broadway* (New York, 1970), Chapter Five, "The Freudian Twenties," pp. 76-96.

21. For a comic version of suppressions, see Susan Glaspell and George Cram Cook, *Suppressed Desires* (1915); for a tragic version, see O'Neill's *Diff'rent* (1920).

22. Richard Cordell, ed., *Representative Modern Plays* (New York, 1930), p. 499.

23. Quinn, II, p. 59.

24. *Ibid.*

25. Crothers, *The Art of Playwriting*, p. 125.

26. *Ibid.*, p. 126.

27. Sievers, p. 80.

28. Flexner, p. 246.

29. John Corbin, *New York Times*, April 17, 1924, Abrahamson, p. 373.

30. The other two plays in this collection include *What They Think*, the scene of the parents' quarrel in *Mary the Third;* and *Peggy*, an uninspired modernization of Crothers's 1902 one-act, *Nora*.

31. Nancy has been active in establishing homes for veterans, a cause with which Crothers was closely and publicly connected between 1918-1921.

32. Burns Mantle, ed., *The Best Plays of 1925-1926*, in Abrahamson, pp. 376-77.

33. Catherine I. Hoobler, "Critics Praise Crothers Play," undated clipping, Crothers Scrapbook, Illinois State University Library.

34. Brooks Atkinson, *New York Times*, December 26, 1927, Abrahamson, p. 378.

35. Krutch, p. 163.

36. *Venus* might prove an exception, but without a complete manuscript it would be difficult to prove.

37. Rachel Crothers, "How Far Does a Girl Go Nowadays," undated reprint of an interview in the *New York World*, Crothers Scrapbook, Illinois State University Library.

38. *Ibid.*

39. Compare, for example, Shafer and "They Stage the Modern Woman," *Pictorial Review*, April 1923, Crothers Scrapbook, Illinois State University Library.

40. "They Stage the Modern Woman."

Chapter Six

1. Morgan Y. Himelstein, *Drama Was a Weapon: The Left-Wing Theater in New York 1929-41* (New Brunswick, N.J., 1963).

2. Malcolm Goldstein, *The Political Stage: American Drama and*

Theater of the Great Depression (New York, 1974). See especially Chapter Six, "Broadway: The Independent Stage, 1930-1935."

3. Flexner, Chapter Seven, "The New Realism."

4. Goldstein, p. 125.

5. *Ibid.*, p. 124.

6. *Ibid.*, p. 126.

7. Crothers, *The Art of Playwriting*, p. 117.

8. Goldstein, p. 126.

9. Flexner, Chapter Six, "Comedy," discusses Crothers, pp. 239-48.

10. Anita Block, *The Changing World in Plays and Theater*, 1939 rpt. (New York, 1971), p. 419.

11. *Ibid.*, p. 3.

12. Statistics from *Best Plays*, cited in Goldstein, p. 126.

13. Flexner, p. 239.

14. Hoobler, Crothers Scrapbook, Illinois State University Library.

15. Arthur Hobson Quinn, ed., *Representative American Plays*, 7th ed. (New York, 1953), p. 895.

16. Baird Leonard, *Life*, March 27, 1931, p. 25, in Abrahamson, p. 390.

17. Francis Fergusson, *Bookman* 73 (May 1931): 296, in Abrahamson, p. 389.

18. Abrahamson, p. 18.

19. Flexner, p. 245.

20. See Winifred L. Dusenburg, *The Theme of Loneliness in Modern American Drama* (Gainesville, Florida, 1960).

21. Filmed in 1940 with a screenplay by Anita Loos, the property grossed over a million dollars from productions in New York and on the road, according to an undated clipping, Crothers Scrapbook, Illinois State University Library.

22. Reported by George Jean Nathan, *Newsweek*, October 25, 1937, p. 25.

23. Richard Watts, *New York Herald Tribune*, October 8, 1937, Abrahamson, p. 406.

24. Stark Young, *New Republic*, October 27, 1937, p. 342.

25. See Watts and Grenville Vernon, *Commonweal*, October 22, 1937, Abrahamson, p. 407.

26. For reference to the range of reviews, see the bibliography for *As Husbands Go*, Abrahamson, p. 383.

27. Hollywood was eager to attract good Broadway dramatists to write literate film scripts. Crothers was one of many New York playwrights who ventured to Hollywood in the 1930s. She adapted her own and others's work for Samuel Goldwyn, her best-known screenplay being *The Perfectly Good Woman* in 1935, with Miriam Hopkins, Billie Burke, and David Niven.

28. Young, p. 343.

29. Helen L. Benson, "Miss Crothers's Play in Paris," *Bloomington Daily Pantagraph*, 1931, reporting on an interview with Crothers by Willis Steell that appeared in the Paris edition of the *New York Herald*. Crothers Scrapbook, Illinois State University Library.

30. Leonard in Abrahamson, p. 390.

31. *Los Angeles Times*, September 14, 1930, in Abrahamson Scrapbook, III, p. 54.

32. Brown's speech is reprinted in Abrahamson Scrapbook, III, p. 67.

33. *Theater Arts Monthly* 15 (May 1931), in Abrahamson, p. 391.

34. Barrett H. Clark, *Drama Magazine* 21 (April 1931), in Abrahamson, p. 388.

35. *Theater Arts Monthly.*

36. Mark Van Doren, *Nation*, March 25, 1931, in Abrahamson, p. 338.

37. "How Great Director Works Told By Writer," *Bloomington Daily Pantagraph*, Dec. 19, 1940, p. 10. Crothers file, Withers Public Library.

38. "Miss Rachel Crothers Busy at Two Jobs in New York City," *Bloomington Daily Pantagraph*, Nov. 24, 1940, p. 11. Crothers file, Withers Public Library.

39. Clipping file, Theater Collection, New York Public Library.

Chapter Seven

1. Djuna Barnes, "The Tireless Rachel Crothers," *Theater Guild Magazine* 8 (May 1931): 18.

2. See, for example, Frame; Lucy France Pierce, "Women Who Write Plays," *World Today* 15 (July 1908): 725–31; Lucy France Pierce, "Women Who Write Real Successes," *Green Book Album* 7 (May 1912): 1058–64; and Helen Johnston Russell, *Social Comment as Depicted in the Plays of American Women Dramatists*, unpublished Ph.D. dissertation, University of Denver, 1958.

3. John Mason Brown refers to Hazlitt's comment in his speech congratulating Crothers for winning the National Achievement Award, in Abrahamson Scrapbook, III, p. 69.

4. Dickinson, pp. 182–87.

5. Quinn, pp. 54–55.

6. Flexner, p. 239.

7. Abrahamson, p. 83, on Gaskell and Jimmie Lee; p. 88 on Remington.

8. John Hutchins, "That Times Square Veteran, Rachel Crothers," *New York Times*, March 15, 1931, Crothers Scrapbook, Special Collections, Illinois State University Library.

9. Rachel Crothers, MS, Letter to Elizabeth Jordan, May 2, [1931],

in the Elizabeth Jordan Papers, Manuscript and Archive Division, New York Public Library.

10. Crothers, *The Art of Playwriting*, p. 117.

11. Rachel Crothers, MS, untitled, unpublished, undated, pp. 3-4, Microfilm, University of Chicago Library.

12. Phillips, Abrahamson Scrapbook, III, p. 59.

13. For examples of feminist plays that are clearly issue-oriented, see Charlotte Perkins Gilman, *Three Women*, a one-act play, in *Forerunner 2* (May 1911): 115-23; 134; and *Something to Vote For*, a one-act play, in *Forerunner 2* (June 1911): 143-53. See also Marion Jean Craig-Wentworth, *The Flower Shop* (Boston, 1912). This full-length play is an explicit argument for woman's economic indepen-dence as well as for suffrage, the shop being the center of a world of independent women as well as those attempting to liberate themselves. Crothers never took up the question of suffrage in her plays, although she personally declared herself in favor of it. See *Woman's Who's Who of America 1914-1915*, ed. John W. Leonard (New York, 1914), p. 218.

Selected Bibliography

PRIMARY SOURCES

Since a chronological list of the plays' publication dates does not reflect the actual chronology of Crothers's output, and since texts of many of the early plays are available only in undated manuscripts, I have noted the date of the first New York performance in parentheses. Mantle's *Best Plays* series provides production dates for all plays except the first three.

1. Plays

Criss-Cross. New York: Dick and Fitzgerald Publishers, 1904 (April 1899).

Nora. Undated manuscript. Burnside-Frohman Collection, The Theater Collection, New York Public Library (Sept. 1903).

The Rector. New York: Samuel French, 1905. (April 3, 1902).

The Coming of Mrs. Patrick. Undated manuscript. Special Collections, Illinois State University Library (Nov. 6, 1907).

A Man's World. Boston: R.G. Badger, 1915 (Feb. 8, 1910).

The Three of Us. New York: Samuel French, 1916 (Oct. 17, 1906).

Myself Bettina. Undated manuscript. The Theater Collection, New York Public Library (Oct. 5, 1908).

Ourselves. Undated manuscript. Rare Book Collection, University of Pennsylvania Library (Nov. 13, 1913).

Young Wisdom. Undated manuscript. The Theater Collection, New York Public Library (Jan. 5, 1914).

A Little Journey. Mary the Third, Old Lady 31 and A Little Journey. New York: Brentano's 1923 (Dec. 26, 1918).

Mary the Third. Mary the Third, Old Lady 31 and A Little Journey. New York: Brentano's, 1923 (Feb. 5, 1923).

Old Lady 31. Mary the Third, Old Lady 31 and A Little Journey. New York: Brentano's, 1923 (Oct. 30, 1916).

39 East. Expressing Willie, Nice People, 39 East. New York: Brentano's, 1924 (March 31, 1919).

Mother Carey's Chickens, with Kate Douglas Wiggin. New York: Samuel French, 1925 (Sept. 25, 1917).

Once Upon a Time. New York: Samuel French, 1925 (Dec. 3, 1917).

The Heart of Paddy Whack. New York: Samuel French, 1925 (Nov. 23, 1914).

Nice People. Representative American Dramas, National and Local. Ed. Montrose J. Moses. Boston: Little, Brown & Co., 1925 (March 2, 1921).

Six One-Act Plays. Boston: Walter H. Baker Company, 1925.

Let Us Be Gay. New York: Samuel French, 1929 (Feb. 21, 1929).

Expressing Willie. Representative Modern Plays. Ed. Richard Cordell. New York: Thomas Nelson and Sons, 1930 (April 16, 1924).

As Husbands Go. New York: Samuel French, 1931 (March 5, 1931).

When Ladies Meet. New York: Samuel French, 1932 (Oct. 6, 1932).

Susan and God. New York: Random House, 1938 (Oct. 7, 1937).

He and She. Representative American Plays 1767 to the Present Day. Ed. Arthur Hobson Quinn. 7th ed. New York: Appleton-Century Crofts, Inc., 1953 (Feb. 12, 1920).

2. Nondramatic Writings

"Troubles of a Playwright," *Harpers Bazaar* 45 (January 1911): 14, 46.

"The Future of the American Stage Depends on Directors," *New York Times Magazine,* December 3, 1916, p. 13.

"The Producing Playwright," *Theater Magazine* 27 (January 1918): 34.

"How Far Does a Girl Go Nowadays," undated reprint of an interview in the *New York World,* Crothers Scrapbook, Special Collections, Illinois State University Library.

"The Construction of a Play," in *The Art of Playwriting.* Lectures delivered at the University of Pennsylvania by Jesse Lynch Williams, Langdon Mitchell, Lord Dunsany, Gilbert Emery, and Rachel Crothers; Foreword by Arthur H. Quinn, 1928, rpt. Freeport, New York: Books for Libraries Press, 1967.

SECONDARY SOURCES

Several collections of documents pertaining to Crothers's career, mainly reviews of her plays and newspaper interviews with Crothers at various stages in her career, are referred to in the notes and references. Some collections are files of clippings; others are scrapbooks, assembled with varying degrees of formality. The principal collections are:

a) Crothers file, clippings from the *Bloomington Daily Pantagraph* from 1893–1958, Withers Public Library and Information Center, Bloomington, Illinois.

b) Three volumes of scrapbooks compiled by Irving Abrahamson contain material collected by Crothers's sister, principally from New York newspapers. The pages of the three volumes are numbered and

cover dates as follows: Volume I—1906-1918; Volume II—1912, 1917-1918,1930-1935; Volume III—1919-1932. These volumes are available on microfilm from University of Chicago Library.
c) The Crothers Scrapbook in Special Collections, Illinois State University Library, Normal, Illinois, contains approximately ninety unnumbered pages of clippings donated to the library by a friend of Crothers.
d) The Robinson Locke Scrapbooks, Theater Collections, New York Public Library, contain an outstanding selection of documents pertaining to the first two decades of Crothers's career. Scrapbooks are organized according to actresses' names, and reviews of Crothers's plays can be located according to the leading lady of the particular play.

ABRAHAMSON, IRVING I. *The Career of Rachel Crothers in the American Theater*. Unpublished Ph.D. dissertation, University of Chicago, 1956. This is the only full-length study of Crothers's plays. I have described it in Chapter 7.

ANONYMOUS. *Theater Arts Monthly* 15 (May 1931), in Abrahamson, p. 391. Castigates Crothers for her use of the "sure-fire formula" in *As Husbands Go* and provides a succinct statement of the values militating against the genre in which Crothers wrote.

BLOCK, ANITA. *The Changing World in Plays and Theater*. 1939; rpt. New York: Da Capo Press, 1971. Particularly critical of Crothers as representative of superficial Broadway amusement.

DICKINSON, THOMAS. *Playwrights of the New American Theater*. New York: The Macmillan Company, 1925. Chapter Three, "Interpreters of the American Scene," section five, devotes pp. 182-88 to a summary of Crothers's career to 1923.

DOWNER, ALAN S. *Fifty Years of American Drama*. Chicago: Henry Regnery, 1951. An analysis of American drama from 1900-1950 which emphasizes the origins and developments of types of American plays and identifies major characteristics of American drama.

EATON, WALTER P. *The American Stage of Today*. Boston: Small, Maynard and Company, 1908. "Our Infant Industry," pp. 6-26, surveys the first decade of twentieth-century American drama, with a view toward encouraging the fledgling native drama.

——. *At the New Theater and Others. The American Stage: Its Problems and Performances 1908-1910*. Boston: Small, Maynard and Company, 1910. "Miss Crothers Champions Her Sex," pp. 155-61, is a thorough and lively discussion of *A Man's World*.

FLEXNER, ELEANOR. *American Playwrights: 1918-1938. The Theater Retreats from Reality*. Freeport, New York: Books for Libraries Press, 1969. Section Three in Chapter Six, "Comedy," pp. 239-48, considers Crothers's earliest and latest plays in a succinct but insightful analysis of the dramas. This analysis has been discussed in Chapter 7.

FORMAN, HENRY JAMES. "The Story of Rachel Crothers: America's Leading Woman Playwright." *Pictorial Review* 32 (June 1931): 2, 56, 59. A gushing portrait, interesting for its apology for Crothers's energy and success and its insistence that her writing on women is in no way "propagandist."

GAGEY, EDMUND. *Revolution in American Drama.* New York: Columbia University Press, 1947. Interesting as a "panoramic survey" of the first four decades of twentieth-century American drama, as well as for considering Crothers's plays of the 1920s.

GOLDSTEIN, MALCOLM. *The Political Stage: American Drama and Theater of the Great Depression.* New York: Oxford University Press, 1974. A valuable general reference, especially the discussion of Broadway's offerings, 1930–1935.

HAMILTON, CLAYTON. *Problems of the Playwright.* New York: Henry Holt and Company, 1917. Chapter 11, "Youth and Age in the Drama," pp. 77–88, gives a favorable account of *Old Lady 31.*

HAPGOOD, NORMAN. *The Stage in America 1897–1900.* New York: Macmillan, 1901. Interesting firsthand account of theatrical conditions and concerns just as Crothers begins her playwriting career.

KRUTCH, JOSEPH WOOD. *The American Drama Since 1918*, rev. ed. New York: George Braziller, Inc., 1957. Refers only briefly to Crothers, but provides a valuable reference for understanding the contribution of popular as well as avant-garde theater in the history of modern American drama.

MANTLE, BURNS, and SHERWOOD, GARRISON P., eds. *The Best Plays of 1909–1919.* New York: Dodd Mead and Company, 1933. From 1920 on, Mantle compiled yearly editions of this series.

———. *The Best Plays of 1899–1909.* New York: Dodd Mead and Company, 1947. Indispensable reference for dates of first New York productions and number of performances of Crothers's plays.

MARSHALL, MARGUERITE MOOERS. "What Do Women Think of Other Women?" *New York World,* 1915, Crothers Scrapbook, Special Collections, Illinois State University Library. Provides a rare discussion with Crothers directly related to feminism.

MILLER, JORDAN Y. *American Dramatic Literature: Ten Modern Plays in Historical Perspective.* New York: McGraw-Hill Book Company, 1961. Excellent bibliographies and chronologies of American drama, particularly for American drama before 1918.

PATTERSON, ADA. "Woman Must Live Out Her Destiny." *Theater* 40 (May 1910): xxiv, 134, 136. Interesting early interview with Crothers that concentrates on her characterization of modern woman.

PHILLIPS, HENRY ALBERT. "Rachel Crothers Talks of Her Plays." *New*

York Herald Tribune, March 15, 1931, Abrahamson Scrapbook, III,
p. 59. Extremely useful retrospective comments by the playwright
on her plays.

PIERCE, LUCY FRANCE. "Women Who Write Plays." *World Today* 15
(July 1908): 725-31; and "Women Who Write Real Successes."
Green Book Album 7 (May 1912): 1058-64. The content of the two
articles tends to overlap, but they describe Crothers's early
achievements in the context of general praise for the emerging
number of women playwrights.

POGGI, JACK. *Theater in America: The Impact of Economic Forces
1870-1967.* Ithaca, New York: Cornell University Press, 1968.
Especially useful for understanding the economics of the American
theater during Crothers's apprenticeship and early works.

QUINN, ARTHUR H. *A History of the American Drama from the Civil
War to the Present Day,* rev. ed. New York: Appleton-Century-
Crofts, Inc., 1936. Vol. 2, Chapter 14, "Rachel Crothers and the
Feminine Criticism of Life," pp. 50-61. This survey of Crothers's
plays, from the beginning to 1925, has been discussed in Chapter 7.

SHAFER, YVONNE B. "The Liberated Woman in American Plays of the
Past." *Players* 49 (April-May 1974): 95-100. Reviews Crothers's
woman-centered plays and discusses them in the context of several
plays from the last sixty years favoring the liberation of women.

Index